MERCENARY MUM

MERCENARY MUM

MY JOURNEY FROM YOUNG MOTHER TO BAGHDAD BODYGUARD

NERYL JOYCE

NERO

The names of certain individuals in this book have been changed for privacy reasons.

Published by Nero,
an imprint of Schwartz Publishing Pty Ltd
37–39 Langridge Street
Collingwood VIC 3066, Australia
email: enquiries@blackincbooks.com
www.nerobooks.com.au

Copyright © Neryl Joyce 2014
Neryl Joyce asserts her right to be known as the author of this work.

ALL RIGHTS RESERVED.
No part of this publication may be reproduced, stored in a retrieval system, or transmitted in any form by any means electronic, mechanical, photocopying, recording or otherwise without the prior consent of the publishers.

National Library of Australia Cataloguing-in-Publication entry:
Joyce, Neryl, author.
Mercenary mum: my journey from young mother to Baghdad bodyguard / Neryl Joyce.
9781863956918 (paperback)
9781922231765 (ebook)
Joyce, Neryl. Australia. Army—Women—Biography. Women soldiers—Australia—Biography. Soldiers—Australia—Biography. Private security services—Employees—Biography. Iraq War, 2003–2011—Participation, Australian—Biography. Australia—Armed Forces—Women—Biography.
355.00820994

Cover design by Peter Long.
Cover photograph by Frances Andrijich.

*Make my enemy brave and strong
so that if defeated, I will not be ashamed.
Coyote is always out there waiting,
and Coyote is always hungry.
Sing your death song and die
like a hero going home.*
NATIVE AMERICAN PROVERBS

*RIP my warrior mates Jay Hunt, Stef Surette,
Chris Ahmelman and Rod Richardson*

PROLOGUE

Everything happens for a reason, so I'd been told. Well, there would want to be a good reason behind all the shit I'd been through in the past twenty-four hours: I'd been fired, burnt and in a car accident. When I arrived back at the team house from the hospital, the guys had already left for Baghdad International Airport (BIAP). I was supposed to have gone with them. Bee, the only other woman on the team, and I hung around our room, talking about how messed up it was working for the company. Jeep, our team leader, was downstairs flipping out. I was certain he was currently plotting yet more ways to make my life a living hell.

As I lay on my bed listing my grievances, Horse, one of our colleagues, suddenly appeared at the doorway. He was deathly white: "The team has been hit."

I felt as though I'd been punched in the stomach. "How did it happen? Is everyone okay?"

Horse told us the team had been stationary on the airport road when it was hit from the side by insurgents. Two of our guys were dead: one died instantly after being shot in the head; the other had been hit in the femoral artery and bled out. A third was fighting for his life. Horse said it could go either way.

I felt dizzy. The first thing that came into my head was that Jeep and Ghost, who led our counter assault team, had killed my mates. They had sent them to their deaths. I'd told everyone it would happen, but no one had listened. My country manager had ignored me. The whole company had ignored me. What did I know? I was only a woman. I had quit working on Red Zone missions a few weeks beforehand, believing my team leaders would get me killed.

I had been right, but I felt no satisfaction. Two precious lives had been snuffed out, and another was hanging in the balance. I suddenly thought of my son, waiting for me at home. If not for the series of freak accidents I'd had that morning, I would have been out on the airport road with those guys. I ran to the toilet to be sick.

I returned to my room. Bee and I analysed and re-analysed exactly how the team must have been hit. No matter how we looked at it, nothing made sense. What had happened out there? Why hadn't they been moving? It was suicide to be stationary on that road. Bee and I cried together. We cried for our fallen mates and we cried for our friend who was fighting for survival in the hospital.

Hold on, I intoned silently. *Hold on for dear life.*

My earliest memory is of having my ears pierced at the tender age of three. I remember sitting on this huge stool in the middle of a crowded shopping centre, and then feeling an intense pain in my earlobe. *God dammit, it hurt.* I screamed so loudly that my younger sister ran away. I didn't blame her; it was her turn next.

My dad was an army infantry officer and the epitome of organisation and order. My upbringing was very strict. Dad held himself to a high standard, and he expected the same of those around him. He rarely showed emotion and always kept a cool exterior. I'd never know exactly how he was feeling – unless, of course, I was in trouble. Then I'd be left in no doubt.

I loved to him death, though. He used to read bedtime stories to me every night. He was terrific at it, and did all the voices. I would imagine Shep, the doggie hero of one of my storybooks, and me going on some fantastic adventures together. It wasn't often that Dad showed me his loving side, but somehow I always knew I was loved.

Mum was the complete opposite: she was openly emotional

and had no problem with showering me in love and kisses. Equally, she had no problem expressing her anger when I had done the wrong thing. Mum had worked as an enrolled nurse, but was a devoted housewife and mother for the best part of her life. She was the most beautiful person I'd ever known. My brother, Ced, was a year older than me, and my little sister, Lil, was a year younger.

Ced was the perfect son. He could do no wrong. He was quieter and more reserved than most boys, and that helped to foster his angelic image in my mum's eyes. I worshipped the ground he walked on too: he was always doing really cool boy stuff. Together we played fighting games, built cubbyhouses, went looking for new species of bugs and ate Milo straight from the tin. I don't think he liked being the only boy. It certainly didn't help that he had a pushy younger sister who followed him everywhere, demanding that he play with her.

While I was very young, my family lived in Papua New Guinea (PNG). My dad had been posted to an army unit in Wewak, on the northern coast. I remember it being very warm and tropical there. I loved being able to swim every day and play in the narrow slice of jungle that was right behind our house.

One day, when Ced was about seven years old, he said he was going exploring in the jungle with a few boys from next door. It sounded like a lot of fun so I decided that I would go too. Well, that didn't go down well with Ced. My brother was so angry. I didn't know why. I wasn't going to annoy him by talking to him or any of his friends. I just wanted to be part of the adventure.

So I followed them. I pushed through dense foliage and undergrowth a few metres behind Ced and his mates. It was exciting to be exploring the jungle like a real adventurer. I fell down in a shallow creek and was caked in mud, but I didn't care: I was having the time of my life. But my brother didn't want some little girl following him around while he played with his friends. He walked faster and faster until I could no longer see or hear him in front of me.

It was a while before I realised that I was alone. All I could see around me was the thick vegetation of the jungle. I burst into tears. I was so upset that my brother had left me behind. It hurt so much to think that I had been rejected – being lost in the middle of the jungle paled in comparison. I stumbled around for ages until finally I could hear voices: "Yaah!"

I came upon a clearing. There was Ced. He didn't look too pleased to see me. His friends were cross too. He told me to go home and leave them alone. He didn't want me poking around in their business. I started bawling, then turned and ran blindly into the jungle, trying to find my way home.

Some time later I emerged from the trees to find myself in our backyard. Mum, horrified at the sight of her dirty, dishevelled daughter, ordered me up to the bathroom. My brother was in hot water by the time he made it home, and was told never to leave me alone like that again. It's the only time I ever recall his getting into trouble. No smacks, no beltings, just a growling from Mum.

I realised that day I was different from boys. I was not their equal: I was a girl. I wanted to be able to explore, to discover new things and to set off on fascinating expeditions too. Why did they have to treat me differently? I was too young to understand what was going on. I just knew that I wanted to do the fun stuff that boys did. And so began my struggle to be accepted in a man's world.

*

My relationship with my sister, Lil, was turbulent. We never agreed on anything or played nicely together. In fact, we got perverse pleasure from seeing each other get in trouble with Mum and Dad, and one sister was always quick to dob in the other if she saw her doing something wrong.

One day my sister was found lighting matches inside the neighbours' house. The front door had been unlocked and she'd just wandered in: this was PNG in the 1970s so home security was not really an issue. Lil was sent to her bedroom for the rest of the day. At dinnertime she was not allowed at the table with the rest of us and had to eat in her room. I was furious. She had been playing with matches only to be rewarded with dinner in bed. It wasn't fair. I wanted to eat dinner in bed too!

So the next day I took the forbidden box of matches and crept over to the neighbours' yard. I sat down with the matches and proceeded to light them one by one. It wasn't long before my dad spotted me. He stormed over and smacked my hands and legs. I was sent to my room and told to await a belting. In my room I grabbed a book and slipped it down my pants. If I was going to get the belt, I wanted some padding. After my father had finished trying to smooth things over with the neighbours, he returned. He opened my bedroom door to find me lying facedown on the top bunk with a blanket over me. Dad pulled off his belt and began winding it around his hand. I knew what was coming next.

Whack! The belt whipped my bottom. The book provided good insulation, and the blanket helped to conceal it. It didn't hurt too much, but I couldn't let my dad know that. I cried out in pretend pain. I must not have been very convincing, though, because he pulled off the blanket to discover the peculiar new square shape my bottom had taken. He was ropeable once he found the book. He whacked me twice more, and this time it did hurt. I cried out for real, huge tears welling up in my eyes. Dad told me that I should have learnt from what had happened the day before.

I couldn't believe my plan had backfired: Lil hadn't got a belting, but I had. I asked about dinner in bed and was told that I wasn't getting any dinner at all. I learnt a valuable lesson that night: older sisters are always expected to 'know better'. Oh, yeah, and never play with matches.

It wasn't the only time my sister and I got into serious trouble. One day I climbed into a cupboard on a mission to find sweets. I spotted an interesting-looking plastic bottle. I shook the bottle and it sounded like lollies rattling. I opened the lid and, sure enough, inside were the most perfect little green sweets. I popped a couple in my mouth and swallowed. They didn't taste very nice, but they looked so pretty that I had to have some more. As I placed another lolly in my mouth, my sister walked in on me. Straightaway I knew the game was up. The only way I could get out of this without Mum knowing was to give Lil some lollies too. So I tapped out a few for her. I didn't want to give her too many, though; I was the one who had found them and, hence, deserved the most.

Lil ate them but didn't like the taste. I had a couple more before giving up. They might have looked pretty but they tasted disgusting. After that, I was quite tired so I decided to take a nap. I went into my mum's room to lie down next to her on the bed, and then I fell asleep. The next thing I remember was Mum shaking me, and a terrible pain in my stomach.

"Don't put your head back. Don't put your head back," I heard someone say.

I was lying on a bed with people standing all around me. There was a bright light shining right in my eyes, but the rest of the room looked black. I started vomiting. I couldn't stop. I couldn't even hold my head up. All I wanted was to go back to sleep.

"Hold her head up or she'll choke on her vomit."

Everything was blurry. I didn't know what was happening. I started vomiting again. *Why are they letting me vomit everywhere?* I noticed a couple of people doing something to my ankle, but I couldn't see what was going on. Then I passed out again.

I awoke several days later in Wewak Hospital. My sister was in the bed next to mine. It wasn't until my parents came into the room that I finally began to understand what had happened: I had been very sick. In fact, I had nearly died.

The cupboard I had climbed into was the medicine cabinet. I had pulled out a bottle of Camoquin and swallowed about five or six tablets. Camoquin is an anti-malarial drug used to treat children. Two months earlier, a child in Adelaide had died after ingesting only two tablets of the adult version, Chloroquine. My mum told me she had been lying on her bed reading a book, when I stumbled into the room and lay down next to her.

I was peaceful for a short time, and then I started frothing at the mouth. Green bubbles oozed from my lips as I complained about a pain in my tummy. Mum rushed into the kitchen and saw the opened bottle of Camoquin on the bench. She spoke to the houseboy, Peter, and told him to watch my brother and sister while she took me to the army Regimental Aid Post (RAP). The RAP was the closest medical facility to our house, and thank goodness army families were permitted to use it in emergency situations. My dad was contacted at work, and he dashed across to the RAP to see me.

After realising that I had overdosed on Camoquin, the medical staff started pumping my stomach. As a consequence of the overdose, my whole body was bloated and the medical staff couldn't find a vein to attach the drip to. They had to make an incision on the inside of my ankle and poke around until they found a vein.

Once I was in a stable condition, I was transported by ambulance to Wewak Hospital. As Mum and Dad drove there, they remembered my brother and sister back at home with Peter. Peter was a local who my parents employed to do odd jobs around the house. When Dad got back to the house, Peter was agitated.

Lil had also started foaming at the mouth, but it was too late for a stomach pump, as the Camoquin had already gone into her system. Dad rushed her to hospital for treatment and, afterwards, the two of us were put in a room together to recover. We slept for forty-eight hours straight before finally waking up to face the world, very lucky to be alive. We had to stay in hospital for a few more days after that, which was torturous for us. There was nothing to do: there was no television, no toys and no books. We started getting on each other's nerves and, before long, we had set our battlelines and declared war. It was then that we were discharged. If we were well enough to be fighting again, I guess we were well enough to go home.

My war with Lil took a back seat after our baby brother, Shannon, was born. He was the most adorable thing I had ever seen. He had really fine white hair and big googly eyes. I used to pretend he was my baby. I even gave him a new name: Willy. He became my new little friend, and I absolutely smothered him with love.

I was very protective of Shannon. His head was on the large side, and I wouldn't let anyone poke fun at him about it. Shannon was born weighing a whopping 4.5 kilograms. The doctors had to use suction to help get him out. I remember my mum swearing she'd never go through that again, that he'd be her last. I loved playing with Shannon so much – making him giggle and blowing raspberries on his chubby tummy – that I couldn't understand why she didn't want to have dozens more.

When I was five I started school in PNG. For most kids, this is a time for learning new things and making lots of friends. For me, it was an introduction to being bullied. I used to catch the school bus to kindergarten each day. I liked to sit right at the back and sing quietly to myself. One of the older boys didn't like my singing – or perhaps he just didn't like me – and he started picking on me. It began with nasty taunts, and moved on to name-calling and threats. Then he started hitting me. The school principal spoke to him about his behaviour, but that didn't stop him. In fact, it only made things worse. The boy continued to hit me on the bus each day. Eventually, he sent me home with a black eye and a bloody nose. Mum was livid. She went straight down to the school and had words with the principal. The kid was finally expelled and my bus trips were safe at last.

I wish that had been my only experience of bullying. We moved to Singleton, a small country town on the east coast of Australia the following year, and that's when the next person to make my life hell came in. I will never forget her as long as I live. She lived a couple of houses down from us. I don't know why, but she hated my guts. She was two years older than me, and happily wielded all the power of an older kid.

Her tactic of choice was to pretend to be my friend. She'd tell me I could play with her and the neighbourhood kids, but then she'd get them all to run away and hide from me as soon as I arrived. She'd raise my hopes that I was one of the gang and then crush them into the ground. It was emotional and mental torture. Once I realised she was never going to accept me as her friend, I stopped falling for her lies. She then began teasing me all the way home on the school bus for what seemed like months.

In Year Two I started getting told off for talking during class and not paying attention. My teacher, Mrs Moore, would slap my forearms, stick tape over my lips and even lock me in the stationery cupboard for being disruptive.

The stationery cupboard was fairly large, but once there were a few naughty kids in it, the space soon filled up. I vividly remember Mrs Moore stuffing me and three of my classmates into the cupboard as punishment for talking in class. The four of us huddled together in the dark, too terrified to speak.

After we'd been released at the end of the day, none of us spoke a word about it to our parents, or anyone else for that matter. If we talked, we risked repercussions. Fear and the threat of violence will always dictate how you respond to a situation. That is when your survival instinct kicks in and logic sometimes goes out the window. As an eight-year-old, it was easier and safer to suffer my teacher's abuse. I didn't think anyone would believe my story about her anyway; I wasn't the most saintly of children back in those days.

It's no wonder I despise bullies to this day. There's nothing that galls me more than seeing people abuse their authority. Even now, I find myself bucking against systems that are blatantly unfair. I guess it's a consequence of being tormented at such a young age. Feeling powerless as a kid can make you into a victim in your adult life, or it can push you to call out injustice when you see it, even if it gets you into trouble.

One day, out of the blue, I changed. I don't know what happened. I just decided that being known as 'the naughty girl' wasn't working for me. Perhaps it was because Mrs Moore was no longer my teacher, or because we were moving to Canberra. Whatever it was, I started to care about what people thought of me and wanted to be the best that I could. I made my bed every day, I did my homework, I cleaned up after myself – I became the perfect daughter. My grades gradually improved, my temperament settled and I became very organised and neat.

Every action has a knock-on effect. The more I became the 'good' daughter, the worse Lil got. The further we moved in opposite directions, the more we fought. We shared a room and this led to many a great battle. My half of the room was immaculate, with my bed made, my clothes folded up neatly in drawers, and my ornaments placed carefully on the dressing table. Lil's side of the room looked like a bomb had hit it: the bed covers were strewn everywhere, her clothes were dumped in piles on the floor, and she always left dirty plates and cups lying around.

When I turned ten, we moved into a new house and I finally got my own room. It was heaven. I had privacy and the freedom to do my own thing without my sister hanging around. On my tenth birthday, I was given the greatest gift an '80s girl could have asked for: a stereo. It was a dinosaur of a machine, with two gigantic ancient-looking speakers, but I loved it. I could listen to the radio, play tapes, and, best of all, put on records. Tapes were so frustrating – you had to keep rewinding or fast-forwarding to get to the song you wanted – but, with a record, you could go straight to your favourite song.

Having a stereo meant I finally had a release: I had music to listen to! *Take 40* and *Countdown* were my favourite programs. I'd tape songs from the radio and then play them over and over. Madonna became my idol, and my wannabe-pop-star fantasy began. I would come home from school and belt out Madonna tunes. Funny, I still come home from work and belt out Madonna tunes.

Regardless of how dreadful my voice was, I'd while away hours picturing myself as a pop star. Dad thought I was ridiculous for imagining I could possibly grow up to be a singer. He would always tell me to focus on getting good grades at school. That wasn't really a problem for me. Every afternoon throughout my teen years, I would come home and, after getting changed and eating something, spend hours doing my homework.

I'd always have music playing in the background while I did my schoolwork. This was a little harder when I had to write essays, as I found I really had to concentrate. But doing maths was always easy – I could happily study while singing along to my favourite records. It's no coincidence that I became very good at the subject. In fact, I would have gone on to become a mathematician, except that my enrolment at uni got stuffed up and I let the opportunity slide by.

When I turned fifteen, Mum broke some major news to us: she was pregnant again! I didn't think women even *could* get pregnant at forty. Mum's announcement came as a shock to everyone. Even the kids at school were surprised. No one in my class had a brother or sister fifteen years younger than them. Mum had not planned on getting pregnant, but termination was not an option. So there we were: a family with four relatively grown-up kids, preparing for the arrival of a new brother or sister.

Naomi was born late in 1988, the bicentennial year. We all thought she was the cat's pyjamas. She had blue eyes, which would sometimes change to green, and caramel-blonde curls that fanned out around her face. Shannon was ten by now, and understandably resistant to being coddled by me. Naomi was perfect for filling his shoes. Mum also took advantage of my love for my baby sister, especially after a long night of breastfeeding. She would often bring Naomi into my room at six o'clock in the morning. I was always really tired, but Naomi was so cute that I just had to play with her.

At age eighteen it was time for me to leave home and start life on my own. So, with a crappy old black suitcase in my hand, I was dropped off at the train station by my dad. I was off to join the army. I caught a train to Sydney and checked into a hotel. I was so excited about my enlistment ceremony the next day I could barely sleep. I would be a soldier – a fully-fledged soldier!

There were a lot of families present for the ceremony. I was a little embarrassed that no one had come to see me sign my life away, but I soon got over it. As I stood up and swore my allegiance to Queen and country, I felt proud and honoured to have been accepted into the army. As I watched the other enlistees pledge their allegiance, I noticed one particular guy who did not blend in. He had bright-red hair reaching halfway down his back. The officer in charge of the ceremony made a point of rolling his eyes and focusing on this guy's long hair. We all knew what was going to happen: that guy was going to lose his long locks the moment he arrived at the recruit training centre. I chuckled to myself, not realising that the exact same fate awaited me.

At the completion of the ceremony, we all piled onto the coach heading to Kapooka, in the Riverina district in New South Wales. All us girls sat together at the back of the bus. Over the next eight hours we got to know one another. We talked about how tough we thought the next three months were going to be. We placed bets on who would be the first to get in trouble and what the reason would be. We compared fitness levels and general military knowledge as we tried to suss out who was prepared for training and who would struggle.

I honestly didn't have a clue what I was in for. You hear how intense an experience it can be, but it doesn't really register until you go through it firsthand. I started to understand exactly how hard recruit training was going to be the moment I got off the bus, though. It was nine o'clock at night when we pulled into the recruit training barracks. The bus stopped, the doors squeaked open and what looked like a bulldog that had taken female human form stormed on board. Now, I am not that easily intimidated, but when Bulldog started barking orders for us to get off the bus quickly, there was no way I was going to dawdle.

In a mad panic, everyone dashed off the bus and lined up in two rows. Bulldog told all the men to "get lost" and to "keep away from the women". She then told us to grab our bags and follow her. All the girls, including me, rushed towards the bus and scrambled around trying to get our bags. It wasn't hard for me to identify my bag: it was the only one that looked as though it had started life in the '70s and then been on a world tour. I grabbed it and tried to keep pace with Bulldog.

I couldn't catch her. I hadn't done much fitness training before joining the army. In fact, I hadn't done much of anything to prepare for recruit training. I thought I'd learn about that stuff once I joined. My bag was heavy and was too antique to have wheels. I was wearing a skirt and high heels and kept stumbling around in the dark. It's a miracle I didn't sprain my ankle. Eventually, I arrived at the building, only to be greeted by two flights of stairs. I dragged my bag up the stairs, then stood at the top, drenched in sweat.

I'd made it, sort of. Then Bulldog's minions swarmed around, screaming at us to get into our rooms. I was placed in a room with three other girls and told to follow their lead. They glanced at me with the same stunned look I was giving them. They didn't have a clue what was going on either. The room was divided in two, with two single beds located in each section. The girl sleeping opposite me was known as Rush Var. In the army, everyone tends to be called by their surname. Maybe it was a ploy by the army to dismantle our identity prior to reshaping it with a new mould? Or perhaps it was just easier to remember one another's surnames because they were displayed on all our clothing and equipment? Either way, my roommate's surname was Rush, and she had three first names. All her equipment was subsequently labelled with Rush VAR, so we started calling her Rash Var instead of her real name. Rush Var was a tall, athletic country girl. She had lived on a farm all her life, and was planning on studying agriculture at uni.

The two girls on the other side of the room were called Putt Putt and Alicia. Putt Putt was a princess: petite and beautiful, with fine blonde hair. She was from the Gold Coast and enjoyed your typical surf-by-day, club-by-night lifestyle. She was planning to study business after her full-time year here. Alicia and I were the same height, but I was about 10 kilograms heavier. She was very outgoing, loved to talk, and refused to be called by her surname. Right from the start Alicia admitted that she wasn't sure she wanted to be in the army. I told her that we were all scared, that no one knew what to expect, and that we'd work it out together. I just wanted her to hang in there and not give up straightaway. The girls all called me "Joycee", and the nickname stuck throughout my time in the army.

"Everyone, get out here now!" The high, piercing yell brought me back to my senses quickly. All the girls came running out of their rooms to line up along the hallway. We weren't allowed to talk or move in any way. We were given detailed instructions about what we were to put in our lockers and how they were to be arranged. We were not permitted to keep any big personal items with us – they had to be left in our suitcases, which would then be locked up in a storage room. We were allowed to keep some small valuables and mementoes in a desk locker, but they had to be left in inspection order. To me, it wasn't worth the extra effort: I packed everything into my bag and that was that.

At ten o'clock it was lights out – regardless of whether we had finished unpacking. I took great pleasure in pulling back the crisp, perfectly white sheets and then lying in my new bed. I was exhausted but couldn't sleep: I was anxious about how I would cope the next day. Eventually I drifted off, but it was a fitful night. I awoke before reveille, not knowing what was going to happen. I didn't even know what reveille was, apart from that it was the time I'd have to get up – 6 a.m. I could hear movement nearby, but no one was getting out of bed yet. *Two minutes before six.* I was counting down. *One minute to go.* Nothing. *Six o'clock.* I held my breath.

"On parade, thirty-two!" screamed the section commanders. *Finally!* I jumped out of bed and lined up in the hallway. 'Thirty-two' was the name of our platoon as well as the shorthand to get everyone to line up 'at attention' in the hallway to await further orders. Forty-five young women stood in various states of dress and disarray, only to be told that we hadn't been quick enough.

We were all sent back to our rooms and into our beds.

"On parade, thirty-two!" they screamed again. Out we jumped again to line up in the hallway. We were better that time; we were more coordinated and a little more awake. But still it was not good enough. The section commanders, or 'seccos' as we called them, explained that recruits often tried to get out of making their beds each morning, so they didn't sleep beneath the sheets. It was the seccos' duty to ensure that everyone slept under their bedclothes. Each morning we were to run into the hallway with both sheets on our shoulders. So we grabbed our sheets and ran into the hallway. Again, we were not fast enough. This game continued for about twenty minutes. We were then given precisely fifteen minutes to make our beds, get dressed, brush our teeth and hair, go to the toilet and then be standing at attention in the hallway again. It was miraculous how fast I eventually became at achieving all this. Even to this day I can still be dressed and ready to go in an instant, so long as you don't judge me on my fashion sense and hairstyle!

My platoon was divided into four sections, and each section was allocated a commander. I was assigned to 'one section', which had Corporal Harty as my secco. Harty was a lean, mean Maori machine; she was also incredibly beautiful. I loved that she could be so tough yet so feminine at the same time. I wanted to be like that too. Harty had recently returned from her honeymoon, after marrying the man of her dreams. I was pretty happy having her as my secco because I thought she might be a little softer on us, given her loved-up experiences over the past couple of weeks. I was wrong: she was a hellcat. I can still hear her penetrating voice echoing through my brain, screaming at me to "HURRY UP!"

*

The next few days were a blur of being issued equipment and clothing. The army gave us everything we could possibly need for the following months: we were issued shoes, uniforms, field equipment and even undies and sports bras. Harty instructed our section on how everything was to be presented in our rooms, including the measurements our clothes had to be ironed and folded into. I couldn't believe I had to get out a ruler to measure my undies, ensuring that I ironed them into the correct dimensions. I then had to place them in a certain position on my shelf, so that they were ready for inspection at any time.

I was only a few days into the training and, so far, it was going well. I wasn't a 'heat seeker' – those poor sorts who were always in the firing line because they had trouble organising themselves. Harty and the other seccos would home in on those girls and grill them until they felt two inches tall. I had managed to avoid that kind of heat – thank God – but I did cry on the fourth day.

Bulldog was working on bringing up our dress standards. She was particularly disgusted by the state of our hair. She announced that there was going to be a 'bun test' and those who failed would have their hair cut off. I was horrified. I didn't think they could make us do that kind of stuff. But they could and did. First, the girls with short hair were inspected and forced to get a haircut if they had 'step cuts' or any other breaches of army dress standards.

The long-haired girls, including me, were then given four minutes to each put up our hair in a neat bun. It only took me a minute. Bulldog inspected my bun and then pointed at my elastic band. I had used a thick pale-green elastic. That particular green was not 'legal'. I was only allowed to use black or brown elastics. Bulldog couldn't have cared less that I did not have any of the right coloured elastics: she told me to borrow one from another girl in the section. Most of the girls didn't have any spare, but eventually I was given a thin black elastic band by a mate. Now, I have some of the thickest hair known to womankind. A weak little elastic like the one I had been given wouldn't hold up half my hair let alone all of it.

Bulldog wasn't interested in excuses. She just wanted results. I struggled with the elastic band and had to use about twenty bobby pins to hold my bun together. After four minutes, I ended up with what looked like a fragile bird's nest at the base of my neck. Bulldog asked me to jump up and down. Within seconds, the bun had fallen out. "Fail!" she yelled. I was devastated. The army works so hard to make you tough and strong and able to cope in an environment dominated by men. You're expected to shoot, run and fight like a man (or get as close as you can to those standards). When my hair was cut off, it was like that last piece of femininity had been taken away from me. I wanted to live and work in a man's world, but not at the expense of my feminine side. So I cried like a girl. I swore it'd be the last time they made me cry, though.

As the weeks went by, I learnt about weapons, first aid, navigation, drill (marching) and section attacks. I was quite good at handling a weapon and one of the best shots in the platoon. Navigating in the bush with a map and compass was a new experience for me, but, once I got out there a couple of times, it was easy. I was often the first to finish navigation exercises and felt proud that I could excel in something. Although I was above average in my other subjects, my poor fitness was starting to detract from my overall performance.

I was hopeless at running. My fitness level was the worst in the platoon. Fitness was the most important aspect of training or, at least, the seccos placed a greater emphasis on it than on anything else. Harty labelled my performance "spasmodic". One day I would be doing really well, then we'd do a fitness session and my standard would plummet again. I didn't know what to do. Even though I would slog my guts out during physical training (PT), I just couldn't keep up with the other girls. I was scraping by in the progressive fitness tests, but then I developed stress fractures in my left foot, which made running extremely painful.

My foot would swell and ache after training hard. So I would rest my ankle overnight, enough for it to settle down so that I could train on it, but afterwards it would blow up again. It was a vicious circle. It was worrying because the fitness tests were gradually getting harder and more sustained. I wouldn't be able to put up with the pain for too much longer. I was edging towards the final stage of my training. I was so close to graduating that I kept pushing myself. There was one more test to complete: the dreaded 4-kilometre run.

The 4-kilometre run test was the bane of my existence. I had attempted it several times before, but was unable to pass. I failed the first test by one minute, the second test by twenty seconds, and the third by two minutes. I was heartbroken. Failing that test meant that I could not complete the training alongside my mates, and that I would be sent to Digger James platoon for remedial training. I would then be back-classed to another, more junior platoon once my foot healed, and I would not graduate with my friends.

My foot and ankle were killing me so I was sent to the medical centre for treatment. There was not much they could do about the stress fractures. The only thing for it was to rest and let them heal naturally. Unfortunately, I didn't have the time to let them heal. I had to keep going. I didn't want to be back-classed to another platoon. But I had no say in the matter. The doctors gave me a chit (a medical advice form) to rest my foot for the next three days, which meant I wouldn't be allowed to do any drill or fitness training.

I returned to my platoon and packed up all my kit. The chit had sealed my fate: I was sent to Digger James. I hugged and kissed my friends goodbye and headed over to Reject Platoon. I sat there for the rest of the day, wallowing in self-pity, polishing my boots and ironing my uniforms.

The next day moved just as slowly. I stayed in my room making everything perfect. I couldn't control my foot, but I could certainly control how my uniform looked and how clean my room was. After lunch, I was called to attention by surprise and told that I had been given special approval to attempt the 4-kilometre run, but that it would be my final chance. If I passed, I would be allowed to return to my original platoon and complete the final stage of training. If I failed, I'd be watching my friends march out of Kapooka from the spectator stands before going back to my spotlessly clean, but very lonely, room.

One of the Digger James staff members came over to say that she'd run with me. She was adamant she'd get me over the line in time, no matter what. She was going to keep to a schedule and get me to points along the course by certain times. I was taken aback by her generosity, and a little jolt went up my spine. My foot was feeling rested and not at all sore; I had someone to motivate me along the way; and there was a strong incentive to pass: I was ready for this.

The physical training instructor (PTI) pulled out his timer as I lined up at the start of the course. *Ready. Set. Go!* I was off. The first part of the run was downhill, so I put on some pace. My motivator stayed close. *One kilometre down.* "Keep it going. You're ahead of time," she panted. The road flattened out and I made it to the halfway point. *Two kilometres.* "You're doing good. Turn around and go back. Don't slow down," she said. I turned at the halfway point and started to head back for the final leg.

Three kilometres. "You're almost there. You're still ahead of time. Push hard and lean into the hill." Running down the hill at the start of the test had been great for pushing ahead of time, but to finish the run by going up it sucked severely. "Shit. I've stuffed up: you're about twelve seconds behind. Pick up the pace, Joycee. You're not going to make it if you don't." It was like a punch to the guts, but I steeled myself. I had to make it. So I ran as though my life depended on it. I could see the finish line in the distance.

My lungs were killing me. My legs felt like lead. I was going to explode. I could feel myself slowing down. *Five hundred metres to go.* All of sudden I heard yelling and screaming: my platoon was cheering me on. They were training at the nearby obstacle course when they saw me make the turn at halfway. Harty had allowed them to come over and show me some support. "Go, Joycee, go!" they shouted out at me. They screamed out words of encouragement as I raced past them. I felt an incredible force from within, pushing me towards the finish line. I didn't want to let them down by failing. I didn't want to let myself down by failing. I was breathing so hard that strange sucking noises started coming from my throat. And then I sprinted over the line.

The girls jumped on top of me as I gasped deeply for air. I was ecstatic that they'd come over to cheer me on, but I still didn't know if I had passed the test. I needed to have finished the run in less than twenty-one minutes. Everyone quietened down and turned to face the PTI. He looked at us all intently, savouring his time in the spotlight. He cleared his throat, then said: "Twenty mins and fifty-nine secs." I'd done it! It wasn't a pretty pass, but it was a pass nonetheless. Everyone cheered loudly, especially me. I'd achieved something that I was proud of. My mates had supported me and I would have done anything for them in thanks.

The girls were then whisked away to complete their obstacle

course, while I returned to Digger James to pack up my gear. I turned and began hobbling away. My foot was throbbing now and my ankle had blown out to twice its usual size. I knew it would be okay, though. I just needed to put some ice on it. I didn't even feel the pain by the time I returned to my platoon. The girls congratulated me on my 'Chariots of Fire' finish, and hugged me as I walked in the door.

I learnt an important lesson through all the difficulties I faced with my fitness: never give up. Never give in when things start getting tough. Don't take the easy way out. Nobody respects a quitter. If you can't keep up, then keep going until you can catch up. That lesson has stayed with me ever since: if you quit, then you are a failure (and Harty will kick your arse for it!).

I was happy to be back with my platoon and among my friends again. There was a concert that night. Each platoon was to put on a performance, and the best act would win $100 for the group. Ours was the only female platoon at Kapooka at that time, and we decided to use our feminine wiles to win the cash. We would put on a fashion parade. On the catwalk, we first had girls dressed conservatively, a representation of how we were when we commenced training. Next, some girls came out dressed a little more daringly, representing the mid point of training. Finally, the really brave girls dressed scantily in bikinis, underwear and night attire: a representation of our confidence levels at the final stage of training. The guys in the audience went crazy at this point. There was never any doubt that we would win the money!

Our act was talked about for days until a rumour started circulating. A guy from another platoon had attempted suicide. He had decided that he didn't want to be in the army anymore, but he was not permitted to leave. It is extremely difficult for a recruit to leave during army training. They won't let you out unless you have a really good reason, and most times you have to be psychologically assessed first. This particular recruit had been discovered slumped over his desk with his wrists slit. We had all heard about people deliberately hurting themselves during PT or even going as far as drinking Brasso cleaning fluid to get out of the army, but this was quite different and very confronting. What made this story even more shocking was that I knew the man: it was the redhead from the enlistment ceremony.

I felt pity for him, but suicide is a loser's way out. There's no thought or regard given to the family and friends left behind. Things can really suck at times, but why would you want to give in? Dig your way out! If you need help, then ask for it. The guy was removed from training and he never returned to his platoon.

The final test before graduation was almost upon us. The 'final fling' was to be the culmination of all our training. It was a three-day field exercise that would test all facets of our military training. The exercise would conclude on the third day with the completion of 'the challenge', which comprised a 15-kilometre forced march, a stretcher carry, an obstacle course, a section attack, a river crossing and the bayonet assault course. It was going to be tough.

As I was in one section, our group would be the first to leave on the challenge. The second, third and fourth sections would leave at ten-minute intervals after us. Harty told me that, if I couldn't keep up with my section, I could drop back and finish it with two section. If I couldn't keep up with them, I could fall back to three section. But if I couldn't finish with four section, then I would fail. I had no intention of falling back at all. I was going to start with my section and finish with them.

I knew my fitness was crap when compared to the other girls', but that was only really evident during running PT sessions. During forced marches, where we marched at a fast pace, I could sort of get by. I knew the girls with shorter legs would struggle during the march, so there was a chance I would be able to keep up. As for the stretcher carry and other military fitness exercises, I was just as strong as the other girls. So I just had to focus on keeping up with the group during the forced march – all 15 kilometres of it.

Meanwhile, the seccos were secretly placing bets on who would pass the challenge and who would give up. Rush Var overhead them talking about it, and came back to report what she'd heard. The seccos had bet that Putt Putt wouldn't make it: she had "short legs" and tended to "psyche herself into failing before she'd even started". Another 'fitness-challenged' girl, Libby, was also pitted to fail, as they thought she "lacked guts" and would give up easily. Then the seccos discussed how they thought I would go.

They could not decide on the outcome. Two of the seccos thought my fitness would let me down, but the other two reckoned my determination would get me over the line. They had been debating it for a little while when finally Harty put her money where her mouth was. She bet that I would make it. I knew inside that she was right: I *could* make it and I knew there was no way in hell I was going to give up. This was my big chance to prove it to myself and everyone else.

It was five in the morning and I was freezing my butt off. I scoffed down a breakfast bar from my field rations and crammed all my sleeping gear into my pack. We'd been out in the field for two and a half days, practising and being assessed on our military skills. It was now time to begin the challenge. My adrenaline was pumping and I was eager to get going. The quicker we started, the quicker we'd finish.

We all dumped our packs in the truck, but kept our webbing, which carried ammunition, food and water, and our weapons for fighting the enemy. We lined up with me at the front. The weakest person was always put at the front so that they could set the pace. We took off, walking the first 5 kilometres in the dark. They were easy. I had no problems keeping a good pace. As I watched the sun rise, I realised I was actually enjoying myself.

At the 7-kilometre mark, things were still going okay. I'd made it through the stretcher carry leg, and still had enough energy to keep going. It was at this point they changed the pace setters. I was told to go to the back; the extremely fit and long-legged Rush Var would now set the pace. I started to falter but kept in there. I saw other girls beginning to struggle as well. For some reason this made me feel good – not because they were suffering but because I could see that I was not the only one hurting. We were all in this together. The realisation gave me the strength to keep going.

Then the bitching started. I was used to struggling during fitness training – it had been the story of my life during recruit training – but this was not so for the other girls. I could hear them from within the ranks, muttering and cursing Rush Var for going so fast. They even told her to slow down (without the section commander hearing), but she wouldn't decrease her pace. I guess she didn't want to get in trouble. Putt Putt couldn't keep up and eventually dropped behind. We were told to leave her: the other section would catch up to her, and she'd finish the challenge with them.

Ten kilometres. We were nearing the finish. We completed the section attack drills and then went on to do the obstacle course. I was really hurting by now. We made our way over a small but steep mountain and the pace didn't seem to lessen. My legs felt like jelly and my foot was aching. I pushed through the pain: we were almost finished. There was just the river crossing and bayonet assault course to go, then a short walk to the finish. The river water was cool and refreshing. I welcomed the relief. Getting onto the bank was quite tricky. I slipped in the mud three times trying to get out of that God-dammed river.

Next was the bayonet assault course. This was going to be the hardest moment of the whole challenge. I was physically exhausted and soaking wet. I had to muster all my anger and energy to propel myself along this course. Without them, I would not make it. It was wet and muddy and there was coloured smoke everywhere as simulated battlefield explosions went off around me. I gathered myself for the final assault.

"Arghhhh, die!" I yelled as I pushed my bayonet into the target, a rectangular hay bale with a corflute picture of the enemy attached to it. I ran towards the next target and plunged my knife deep into it. Everything became a blur: the yelling, the screaming, the explosions. I leopard-crawled my way through the mud, jumped over the wire obstacles and stabbed all the targets I came into contact with. Finally, I caught up to the rest of the section. Excited and happy, we were all stepping up the pace now. We rolled across the finish line as a team.

We waited for the other three sections to come in. I hoped that everyone had made it, but it was not to be. Putt Putt had started hyperventilating around the 10-kilometre mark and had to be taken to the med centre. Libby hadn't even reached the 3-kilometre mark. I couldn't understand why. I was the platoon's slowest runner and the weakest in terms of cardio fitness. If I could make it, then surely everyone could. I guess it came down to whether you psyched yourself up, or psyched yourself out.

With that, recruit training was over. I'd passed everything and would graduate in a week's time. The hardest part of my army life was done; everything would be downhill from now on. I couldn't have been more wrong. Recruit training was a cakewalk compared to what I would eventually have to deal with, although it did help to prepare me for some tough obstacles I would face later in life.

We had been marching all week, practising our drill movements until everyone had a 'Kapooka smile' burnt onto their faces. The Kapooka smile was the result of standing in the hot sun all day, every day in our wide-brimmed slouch hats. The hats protected most of the face but somehow the chinstrap area would always be exposed, leaving a suntan mark that stretched across both cheeks. I was proud of my Kapooka smile, as were the other girls. It signified that we were almost bona fide soldiers.

Drill week had been long and exhausting. During the day we practised formations, weapon drill, marching in time and standing still for long periods of time. Of an evening, we would busily prepare our uniforms. Our brass belt buckles had to sparkle, our boots had to be polished until you could see your reflection in them, and our uniforms had to be starched and ironed to perfection. The girls were thrilled at the thought of soon seeing their families who would be coming to watch them officially graduate and march out of Kapooka. I was excited about finishing too, but the parade was just a formality for me. My family wouldn't be there. While I'd been in training, my parents had moved to Cairns. It was just too far away for them to come.

Graduation day arrived. There was anticipation in the air. We dressed carefully and inspected each other for faults. We had to be particular about our appearance and ensure our mates were also immaculately presented. We filed through the armoury to get our weapons, then lined up in three ranks to await inspection. Harty picked over my uniform one last time. I had to be perfect. We all had to be perfect. We were Australia's newest soldiers.

Satisfied that we were up to scratch, Harty took command and marched us down to the parade ground. The spectator stands were full. It wasn't just our female platoon marching out today; there were also four male platoons. I was excited and happy to be leaving. I knew that I had achieved something great. Physical fitness was my biggest challenge, but I had overcome my weaknesses and passed. I knew I deserved this day, although I was a little disappointed not to be able to share it with my family.

It was about 28 degrees Celsius on the day of our graduation in April that year, but on the hot bitumen parade ground, it felt about 40 degrees. During the ceremony everyone was sweating profusely. The girl standing next to me, Smithy, leant over and whispered, "Joycee, I think I am going to pass out." *Oh, no*, I thought. We weren't even halfway through the parade. We still had to stand at attention for some time yet; there were many more speeches to listen to. I had to keep Smithy on her feet. There are not many things that are more embarrassing for a soldier than passing out on parade, especially when it's your own graduation.

Smithy started to sway. "Wriggle your toes and take deep breaths," I whispered to her. It was the standard thing to say, but I hoped it would keep her upright. For the rest of the parade I did my best ventriloquist act. I didn't want to be obvious about talking on parade (a big no-no), but there was no way I was going to let her fall. After all the moral support and encouragement my mates had given me during those harsh physical training sessions, the least I could do was to stop Smithy from fainting on parade. I whispered all kinds of stuff to her. I tried to keep her focused on what I was saying, quite a feat when you can't move your lips.

Smithy made it through all the speeches and got her composure back once we started marching around the parade ground one final time. At the end of the ceremony, we headed over to the boozer for a barbecue and drinks with the families. A few of us congregated at a small table to down Southern Comforts and Coke. We were the orphans, the ones with no family or friends present. We consoled each other over numerous drinks and shared horror stories about our time as recruits.

Smithy came over later that day and bought me a drink. She thanked me several times for talking to her on parade and stopping her from fainting. She then told me that her mother wanted to know why the girl standing next to her daughter had talked the whole way through the parade. I guess I was no ventriloquist after all!

The rest of the day was a haze. I went to bed early that night. I had packed up all my kit and was ready to leave the next day for my next lot of army training: I'd be attending a dental assistant course. I'd be the only one from my platoon; the rest were going off to be army medics, truckies and clerks. I don't know how I ended up choosing that course. Who joins the army to be a dental assistant? I wanted to do all the cool stuff I'd seen soldiers do in action movies, but was instead destined to suck the slag out of people's mouths.

The next morning I walked outside my building to where four buses were lined up. They'd be taking all the newly promoted privates to the sites of their initial employment training: technical schools in Puckapunyal and Portsea in Victoria. I waved goodbye to my friends and watched the buses until they disappeared around the corner. It was hard watching everyone leave.

I was left standing alone. My employment training was to be conducted at the Royal Australian Air Force (RAAF) base down the road. Not knowing what else to do, I walked back to my room. On my way, Harty stopped to ask me if I knew what was happening with my travel. I said I didn't know.

She asked me to wait in my room while she made me a coffee. She'd then go to find out what was happening and get back to me. I was shocked. Harty wasn't speaking to me as though I were the scum of the Earth, lower than low, as she had when I was a recruit. I was a private now, and that meant she could speak to me as she would a normal person. It was really weird. I knew that our treatment during army training was not indicative of life afterwards, but the transition was still extremely unsettling.

I sipped on my hot coffee, trying to calm my nerves. I sat in my room for more than two hours, too afraid to go wandering around the barracks. Even though I wasn't a recruit anymore, I wasn't going to risk getting a bollocking. Eventually, Harty came to get me and my kit: it was time to go to the Wagga Wagga RAAF base.

I knew from the moment I started the dental assistant course that it was not for me. I didn't mind studying the theory and science behind dental procedures, but the applied side of the work just didn't do it for me. Although I passed the theory and practical tests with ease, the incentive to excel just wasn't there. Dental nursing is great for those who enjoy working in a medical environment, but it wasn't what I had joined the army to do. I knew that what I was really after was something that would challenge me. It was one thing to recognise that I wasn't cut out to be a dental nurse, but another to go from bad breath and cavities to a job where the action was.

After six months I had finished all my training. A fresh-faced nineteen-year-old, I was posted to Brisbane, which was where all my recruit mates were being sent as well. As soon as I arrived at the airport, I was picked up by Ranch. Ranch had trained as a truckie after her time at Kapooka, and was posted to my dental unit as a driver. I was ecstatic to see her. It meant that I had at least one friend in my unit.

I asked her what kind of driving tasks she was getting to do in the unit, and she told me she'd been stuck with all the mundane ones. She had to drive a HiAce van around the base completing admin tasks for the unit, like picking up the mail. *What a waste!* I thought. She didn't get to do any of the cool stuff the male truckies did, like drive giant Unimogs around the place.

Ranch was excited that we would be in the same unit. The dental unit was quite small compared to infantry company's, so we'd be able to see each other during PT sessions and our lunch hour. Ranch drove me over to our accommodation, explaining that she and I would be sharing the unit with two other girls. We each had our own room, but we'd be sharing the bathroom and common room. It was like share-housing with three friends. I felt so grown up.

I had arrived on a Friday evening, and Ranch was determined to show me around Brisbane. I barely had time to unpack before she took me out nightclubbing. We went to the local army hangout in the city called 'The Pit'. The place was throbbing with army guys and civilian chicks, all trying to pick up. It was a great way to start life in a new city. I bumped into all my friends and got to hang out and be dickheads with them.

The next day Ranch took me out again. She showed me where the Brisbane markets were, took me to some cool scenic spots, and then we went grocery shopping. The army provided all our meals for us, but we still needed to buy snacks. Towards the end of the weekend, I started to get nervous. The next day I would be starting work as a dental assistant. I would be meeting new people and adjusting to a new environment. Thank goodness Ranch would be there with me. It would make things far less scary.

The next morning Ranch and I walked down to the dental unit. Ranch introduced to me to Corporal Hudson, who looked about fifty years old but was probably only about thirty. Hudson took me on a tour of the unit and introduced me to the other staff. He then informed me that I would be assisting the boss of the dental unit. My heart sank. I was just a private and really didn't know that much about dentistry. Sure, I could perform basic procedures, but there were about a hundred more complex ones that I didn't know a thing about. I couldn't believe they would pair the most junior dental assistant with the most senior dentist.

Sure enough, all my fears were realised. It was absolutely horrible working for the head dentist. He expected me to know much more than I did, and would embarrass me in front of patients if I didn't know the answers to his questions. My days were full and demanding. In the mornings, I would get into work really early to set up the surgery for the day. I'd then have to rush off to smash out a session with the PTIs. When that was over, I'd have to be showered and changed in time to see the first patient at 9 a.m. There was normally just enough time to do this, but I was stuffed if PT went on even a few minutes longer than usual. I'd hear the dentist yelling from outside the bathroom for me to hurry up. The dentists never did PT with our unit, so they were always ready to begin before us.

Then, from the moment I saw the first patient, I would not get a break until the day was over. The scheduled morning-tea break was for everyone except dental assistants. In that time I was expected to have cleaned the dental instruments, sterilised the surgery and prepared for the next patient. I was also expected to catch up on the surgery's paperwork: filling in the patients' medical documents and filing them away at reception.

Even lunchtime was no break. Once again, I was expected to have completed all cleaning before I was allowed to leave. At four in the afternoon, when everyone else had knocked off for the day, I was left there, cleaning instruments, sterilising the surgery and locking up the building. I hated it. It sucked not knowing enough about dentistry. Not being offered more training made it even worse. I spent that six months feeling unsure about my work and terrified of saying the wrong thing to my boss. And there was nothing I could do about it.

My social life helped to get me through. All my girlfriends used to go out clubbing on Thursday and Friday nights. Thursday was ladies' night at The Pit, so my friends used to get free drinks and free entry. I couldn't go with them. I had to be stone-cold sober when I worked. I just couldn't afford to be hung-over in that stressful surgery environment. But every Friday night I partied with them till the wee hours.

I did a lot of growing up and experienced a lot that year. I'm glad I shared that time with a group of such close friends. It is important to have good friends to make mistakes with. Ranch was my best friend and I could tell her anything. We talked about boys, sex, our futures and clothes. That year would have been a hell of a lot worse if she hadn't been there.

It was nearing the end of the year, and shortly I would leave for Cairns to have Christmas with my family. Before that, I had my first bush trip with the dental unit. I had no idea what to expect. The only bush experience I'd had was in those few short days during recruit training, so another dental assistant named Charlie took me under her wing. She showed me how to pack and store the medical supplies, and what quantities were needed for the duration of the exercise. It was going to be a two-week trip in a place called Shoalwater Bay, on the Capricorn Coast in Queensland.

We left early in the morning after bundling into the back of a Unimog. It was squashy, cold and not very comfortable, but I can sleep anywhere. I made myself at home on the packs that were scattered around the floor. I slept until we arrived – a full eight hours. On our arrival, I helped to unpack all the dental equipment. Over the period of a day I learnt what a camouflage net was and how the sticks and mushroom heads are used to hold up the net. Most importantly, I learnt that camouflage nets always go up before the tent. It's never the other way around – unless you want to make things extremely difficult for yourself ... which is what happened on my first attempt.

Little by little, Charlie showed me how to set up a field dental surgery. It didn't take long before we were ready to start seeing patients. I wasn't worried about working in the surgery during the bush trip. I had been assigned to a brand-new dentist (one straight out of training) and knew that complicated dental work would not be attempted in the field.

The two weeks breezed by. I got along with the dentist. We mainly performed annual dental assessments, but also did some fillings and mouthguard impressions. I still had other duties to take care of, such as digging, garbage disposal and water collection. All in all it was very enjoyable. I even got to be on the standby team for emergency response.

Our dental unit was located with the medical unit. It had an emergency response team, which included stretcher-bearers, set to react to any mass-casualty situations. A mass-casualty situation is where there is an influx of patients who all require immediate medical support at the same time. The stretcher-bearers are used to move patients around the field hospital and to support the medics. I was excited to be placed on the roster, even though it was considered by most to be a chore rather than a privilege.

The medical unit ran an emergency drill one day, to make sure we were prepared and able to react quickly. As soon as I heard the siren go off, I grabbed my webbing and weapon, and ran over to the triage point. From then on I was drawn in to another world. I sprinted around, moving patients and helping medical staff. I became acutely aware of everything going on around me and looked for ways to help. I was having the time of my life.

I was sent back to dental and raved on about the experience to Ranch. She thought I was an idiot for getting so excited about it, but

I loved being in an emergency situation and having to react accordingly. Later that night, Corporal Hudson came over to congratulate me on my efforts. The medical staff had been impressed and wanted their thanks passed on. I was happy to have their acknowledgment of a job well done. After spending six months as a sucky (excuse the pun) dental assistant, I was starting to think I was a failure at anything related to medicine. It was just the morale boost I needed.

I'd enjoyed my first bush trip with the dental unit, but not enough to want to stay on as an assistant. With a full-time year behind me, my service to the army would now become part time. I wanted to come back after Christmas for my part-time service – I was keen on the money and seeing my friends again – but the thought of another year of staring into people's mouths in the surgery made me feel sick. I would be returning in January, after the Christmas break but didn't know for how long. I loved the army, but I just wasn't getting to do any of the fun stuff.

In early January 1994, I returned to Brisbane for my part-time service. Hundreds of reserve soldiers had gone home on leave and were now returning for work, money and a hell of a big reunion. The nightclubs of Brisbane were overflowing with soldiers, all looking for a good time.

My first week back at the dental unit mainly involved packing and repacking medical stores. The days were long and boring. I could not keep working as a dental assistant – it wasn't who I was inside. I needed something more than suction machines and dental floss to spike my interest and enthusiasm.

One day, the military police (MPs) came to our medical facility to give us a presentation on their roles in the field. I was absolutely fascinated by everything they said. They announced that they were going to start a new MP platoon, which was to be filled with army reserve soldiers. I knew it was for me. From the moment they showed up in their MP vehicles, tactical belts and bright-red berets, I'd known it was for me.

I begged Corporal Hudson to let me do some on-the-job training with them. He spoke to the MP commander and organised for me to stay with his crew for a few days while they conducted an MP exercise. I was to leave immediately. I packed up my kit in about two minutes flat and carried it over to their vehicle. Sergeant Hanes introduced himself as the MP section commander. He would be the one looking after me while I trained with them. The MPs were keen to have me, as they were always short on staff, and were eager to meet a prospective addition to their new platoon.

Over the next three days, I learnt about traffic control points, prisoner of war facilities and how to conduct a route reconnaissance. The MPs gave me basic lessons on handcuffing and ASP baton use. I loved every second I had with them. I knew that it was the corps I was destined to join. As a woman in the army at that time, I just wasn't able to join combat-related corps. However, as an MP, I'd be able to see and do many things that most women in the reserves wouldn't.

My mind was made up: I was going to apply for a corps transfer to military police. The dental staff had no choice but to recommend the move. I was going nowhere as a dental assistant. Sergeant Hanes provided a favourable report for the time I'd worked with them in support of my application. Before I knew it, my paperwork was signed off and my interviews and testing for the corps were complete. It was time to kiss my dental service goodbye – the next time I came to Brisbane for my army service, I would be going to the MP training school.

*

I returned to Cairns to start a university degree. I got a part-time job at Woolworths and moved into a tiny unit. I loved that little studio apartment and the freedom it afforded me. During my uni breaks, I would fly down to Brisbane for my army reserve training as a member of the MP. I had to work hard to balance the demands of my studies with those of my job, but my life was great. I had everything going for me.

It's funny how when you're on a good run you think things are only going to get better. You don't stop to think that things can go wrong. Why should you? But it doesn't take much to derail someone's life. It could be a car accident, or tripping down the stairs, or a bout of illness. For me, it was falling in love for the very first time.

It was love at first sight. From the moment I saw him I was smitten. His name was Joe. How could I have possibly known that Joe was destined to destroy my soul? I was naive and stupid. There's no other way of explaining it. I was a young woman with minimal experience with men. The only thing I knew about relationships was what I had learnt from my parents. I always believed the best about people and never once considered that someone might mean me harm.

Joe was a Maori, and handsome, athletic and funny. He loved his sport and was extremely loyal to his family and friends. Joe had an identical twin brother, Paul, who happened to be gay. They looked completely different: it was hard to believe they were brothers, let alone twins. Paul was well groomed and always looked immaculate. He plucked his eyebrows, sang in drag and had a lovely, kind heart. If he hadn't been gay, then he definitely would have been the better twin to date!

Joe and I started living together shortly after we'd started seeing each other. I never actually asked him to; he just sort of moved himself into my flat. Joe worked as a cleaner at a luxury resort. He made beds, cleaned bathrooms and occasionally worked as the pool boy.

When Joe moved in, I was surprised to learn that he smoked marijuana. Every day after work, he would come home and light up a joint. I hated drugs and I hated watching him smoke. At first I was afraid to tell him how much his smoking annoyed me. It wasn't as though it was affecting our lives or having any negative impact, but I hated it because it was illegal and went against everything I believed in. I just couldn't be around him when he lit up, and I'd have to leave the house.

Lil had developed a drug problem over the years, so I knew how bad things could get. Admittedly, Lil had moved on to worse things than dope. She was into hardcore drugs: heroin, valium and God knows what else. She was trying hard to get clean but every day was a battle. She started a methadone program, but it was not a cure. Even today she still has a fight on her hands. Once you're hooked, there will always be a monkey on your back. Addiction lasts forever.

I should have finished with Joe the moment I saw him light up. But I stuck with him, hoping I could change him. Over the next few months, Joe's smoking steadily increased. One joint turned into two and, eventually, into too many to count. Ten minutes of smoking turned into a whole evening. And then he started inviting his friends around. He and his mates would cram into my studio apartment to smoke marijuana for hours. They'd play their gangster rap and Bob Marley tunes, and reminisce about the good times they'd shared back in New Zealand.

Joe would talk about the fights he'd got into back when he was in the Bloods gang in New Zealand. I was shocked to learn that every Friday night he used to go out with his gang mates, looking for fights. How could I have fallen in love with a person like that?

But at the same time as he'd boast about fighting, he would get all emotional and talk about how much he loved his family and how he would do anything for them.

Joe's smoking only got worse as time went on. I told him constantly that I hated it and wanted him to quit. Every single time I broached the subject, he'd promise me that he would stop. And stupidly, I believed him. He eventually lost his job at the resort and began collecting welfare payments. I was still working at Woolies, studying at uni, and going back and forth to Brisbane for my army reserve service. The army was a lifesaver. It provided me with an escape from all the negativity in my life.

During the uni holidays, I would return to Brisbane and focus on my military career and spend time with my army friends. I would arrive at my army unit a mess, and then leave feeling happy and self-assured. The time away from home allowed me to regain my strength and confidence. I could actually feel Joe's hold on me slipping, and my old self returning.

Each time I came home from my army service, Joe and I would break up. But after a short time, he would somehow wheedle his way back into my life. Why did I let him? I knew he was bad for me, but still I would not give up on him.

Then I began worrying about what Joe was getting up to while I was away from home. Was he selling our possessions for drugs? Was he rifling through my drawers to find the rent money that I'd hidden? Was he selling drugs out of my home? The questioning was tearing me apart. I pleaded with Joe to get help, but nothing changed. My studies began to suffer, and eventually I stopped attending. I couldn't trust him alone in the house. I knew that things could not continue like this. That *I* could not continue like this. And yet, I couldn't break away for good.

Then came the incident that prompted me to act. Joe's ex-girlfriend, Carla, was dating one of his close dope friends, Jake. They were at our house, once again smoking. Carla was five months pregnant. Although she was a regular dope smoker, she'd cut down quite a bit since finding out she was going to have a baby.

At some stage during the night, Jake and Carla got into a fight. Then Jake started hitting Carla. I told Joe to stop his friend. I was concerned for both Carla and her unborn child. I could tell Joe was uncomfortable, but he simply said that he could not interfere with what his "bro" was doing. It was "none of his business". Carla fell to the ground and curled up, trying to protect her stomach. Jake then kicked her. I felt sick. I couldn't stand by and let this happen. Jake was a big man with a fierce temper, but I didn't care.

I shielded Carla's body with mine. I felt Jake's foot connect with my back. I groaned. It was at this point that Joe finally intervened. Things calmed down, and Jake left. Carla was crying and thanking me all at once. I told her she needed to go to a doctor to get herself and her baby checked out. She assured me she would but that she really wanted to see Jake. I couldn't believe that she was considering going back home to him. He'd just abused her. But several minutes later she left to find him.

I was shell-shocked. Joe had stood by and watched his mate beat up his ex-girlfriend. He had only reacted because I'd literally thrown myself into the fight. How could I love a man who could witness that and do nothing?

The drugs had changed Joe completely. He used to be a fun, sporty guy. Now he was someone with no motivation or self-respect. All he cared about was getting his dole money and spending it on drugs. All of his mates were the same. They bludged off the dole, bludged off each other and their loved ones, and their plans didn't extend beyond smoking weed until they passed out on the floor. I realised that Joe would never change.

I was trying to be a good person, sticking by Joe through the rough times, but this was ridiculous. I was working at Woolies, failing uni, doing my army service and supporting Joe and his drug problem. Two years had gone by and I was a shadow of the person I once was. I was going nowhere.

I decided to make some changes. Joe returned home late one night after smoking and drinking at Jake's place. He looked at me and could tell that something was up. He asked me what was going on. I told him that I was going to become a career soldier and join the army full time. He looked at me in horror, as though he couldn't believe what he was hearing.

Now it was Joe's turn to beg: he implored me not to join. He pleaded with me to keep on working at the Woolies' check-outs. I told him that I wasn't leaving him: he'd be coming with me. I explained that this was our chance to start over, to get away from the dope scene and the bad crowd in Cairns. But he wasn't happy. He was afraid that I would leave him once I joined the army full time. I tried to reassure him that it wouldn't happen, but I knew deep down that he was right. Perhaps that was why I was so determined. I knew that spending time in the army would give me back my dignity and self-respect. I knew that if I worked hard and interacted with good, loyal friends that I would regain the strength to dump this loser and get on with my life.

And then I realised I didn't even need to wait till then. I was finally strong enough to tell Joe that I thought he was a useless, drug-smoking, dole-bludging waster who should be deported. I told him that even though he thought of himself as some kind of Maori warrior, boasting about his fights and cunning tactics, in reality he did nothing but disrespect his culture and the people he loved.

Two years of my life had been wasted on a good-for-nothing druggie. And as much as I blamed him for his addiction, I blamed myself, too, for not having left him sooner. I found myself thinking about Carla, who stayed with Jake after he beat her up. Joe might not have physically abused me, but it was emotional abuse. How could I have let him lower my confidence so much that I wasn't able to leave him? Was I afraid that no one else would love me, that I wasn't good enough? Was I a victim of 'treat them mean, keep them keen'? Or maybe I just foolishly believed I could save him from himself.

Whatever the reason, I was finally able to break free of his hold. I was going to make a fresh start. No more worrying about drugs. No more loser boyfriend. No more financial worries. No more university. No more of the old life. The real me was busting out. I felt like a butterfly finally escaping the confines of a cocoon. Freedom at last!

My life was back on track. The army accepted my application to transfer to full-time service; however, I was required to attend the MP basic course again. I thought it was a waste of time, as I'd already completed all the reserve components of the course, but if I had to do it again, so be it. In the end, I just considered it a good way of cementing everything I knew.

I was excited and motivated, keen to do well in the course and to enjoy myself at the same time. The MP course was to be conducted down in Sydney over three months, with the first part devoted to participants getting their military driver's licences. I already had my licence so I went along as a helper and general dogsbody. I was happy to be there; I felt confident that I had made the right decision about what to do with my life.

What happened next was the very last thing I'd been looking for. I literally fell for Bruce. I was using a payphone on base to call my mum. When I'd finished talking, I stepped out onto the pavement and nearly ran into this guy who was waiting to use the phone. Because I'd stopped so abruptly and then misjudged the step down out of the booth, I tumbled over, landing ungracefully on the ground. I twisted my ankle in the process and felt like an absolute klutz. What an impression I must have made. Bruce helped me up and then took me over to the medical facility, and the rest is history.

I'd had so much stress and worry with Joe, I wasn't sure I could go through all that again. But when it came to affairs of the heart, I was absolutely hopeless. I don't know what it was that attracted me to Bruce the most. Was it his blue eyes and cropped blond hair? Or his exceptional sporting abilities? I think more than likely it was that he was not a drug-smoking, dole-bludging liar. Bruce was a normal guy. He did normal things like work, ring his mum, play sport and have two-way conversations. I wanted normal. I craved normal. And that is what I got.

I studied hard throughout my MP course. I wanted to prove to myself that I could concentrate on my studies while having a relationship. Well into the night, I'd be up memorising paragraphs of text, word for word. I aced all my tests and kept on the instructors' good sides. In fact, I even started to get a little full of myself.

One of my instructors, Leo, was an incredible athlete. He was an awesome runner, boxer and rugby player. He was known as Leo the Legend. He was a great instructor with a terrific sense of humour, but his best quality was his ability to motivate others. Each day at PT he would wear this cap that had the word 'coach' emblazoned on it. He was proud of his cap because the rugby team he was coaching at the time had presented it to him as a gift.

One day, Leo left his cap in our dining hall. It is customary to take off your hat in an army dining hall and place it on a rack. On this particular day, he forgot to retrieve it after he'd finished eating. It was then that I hit on a plan: the cap would be held for ransom. I grabbed the hat from the hook and hid it in my bag.

When classes were over for the day, I conspired with my course mates. Together we taped a sign with the word 'slow' to the cap so that it read 'slow coach' – a swipe at Leo's running ability. We took photos of the cap at various places around the base, and then wrote a ransom note to Leo: "We have your hat! You're not getting it back."

Over the duration of the course we sent photos of Leo's hat to him. His cap went to Manly Beach; it found itself at nightclubs, pubs, restaurants and out on our final bush trip. Towards the end of the course, Leo and the other instructors came into our classroom to inform us they were going to conduct a room inspection. We all knew that what they were actually attempting was a search-and-rescue mission for the cap. The instructors left to attend to some admin. Meanwhile, we were forbidden to leave the classroom.

As soon as the instructors left, I told everyone that the cap was sitting in plain sight on my bed. As soon as they entered my room, the game would be up. My mate Warne said he would race to my room, grab the hat and hide it. I didn't think he'd make it in time. He grabbed my room key, sprinted off and got back thirty seconds before the instructors walked into the classroom. He'd done it!

The instructors conducted the inspection but did not find the hat. They threatened to detain us until the cap was released, unharmed. I could see a couple of my course mates were about to break down and reveal all (they would have missed out on an episode of *The Simpsons* or something), but the instructors ended up letting us go. The search only fed our appetite for fun. We stepped things up, sending him ever more outrageous letters and photos.

On the final day of the course, my friends and I relented. We stuck copies of all the photos we had taken onto a board, which we presented to Leo. We thanked him for his instruction and guidance during the course, and then, finally, gave him back his cap. He was touched. He put up the board in his office. We would be remembered as his favourite ever students. (Okay, I made up that last bit, but I'm sure he had a soft spot for us in the end.) I had got so much out of the MP course and, to top things off, I was named the student of merit.

I was surprised but happy. I'd studied really hard and done well on all my tests. I'd gone from being a Woolies check-out chick with a deadshit boyfriend to being my course's top student, with a promising future and a normal relationship.

In addition, I had been given my posting order: Townsville. I was ecstatic. Not only did it mean that Bruce and I would be working near to each other, but also I'd have the opportunity to join the rapidly deployable force. I loved the idea of deploying at short notice to unstable countries. It didn't particularly worry me that I was the only woman in the MP platoon. In fact, it would come to work in my favour.

It began with a knock on my door. I'd just finished getting dressed in my PT kit and was about to head off to work on my trusty pushbike. I opened the door to see Butts, a colleague who also lived in the dormitory. He told me he'd just received a phone call from the platoon commander. I didn't own a mobile phone at the time, so the platoon commander had rung Butts to pass on a message to me ASAP: I was to report to 4 Field Regiment (4 Fd Regt) in fifteen minutes' time.

Whoa! What was going on? Butts had a car and told me he'd give me a lift there. I quickly changed into my uniform and jumped in his car. He drove through the 4 Fd Regt gates and dropped me off in front of the main building. I got quite a few curious stares from unit members; my bright-red beret made it difficult for me to blend into the surrounds. Luckily, I wasn't there for long before more MPs turned up. The second-in-command of my section, Corporal Murphy, and another section member, Corporal Monroe, entered, making us a party of three. They had also been told to report to 4 Fd Regt, and did not know what was going on either.

Murphy went into the headquarters and motioned for us to

follow him. We sat down at a table inside a briefing room. Within a few minutes, the room was filled with various artillery commanders. We were then told to prepare ourselves for immediate deployment to Cambodia: we were going to assist with evacuating Australians and some foreign nationals from the country.

I couldn't believe what I was hearing. I was excited to say the least. I had only been in the unit a little more than a month, and now I'd be deploying on a real operation. I didn't have a clue what was going on in Cambodia. I'm not sure I could have even pointed to it on a map. Geography had never been my strong suit.

After the briefing, the three of us returned to our unit and immediately began sorting through our field equipment and personal issues. Our operation was deemed secret so we were only allowed to inform our families that something was going on and that we were required to deploy somewhere at short notice. I rang Mum to let her know I was going away, but that I couldn't tell her anything about it. I told her to watch TV and put two and two together. I then rang Bruce to let him know the same.

At 9 a.m. that same morning we had to return to 4 Fd Regt with all our kit. We were then issued additional equipment: Kevlar helmets, body armour, ration packs and so on. By then, I had listened to a few radio reports. The Cambodian Second Prime Minister, Hun Sen, had launched a coup against the First Prime Minister, Prince Norodom Ranariddh. The country had subsequently fallen into chaos. We were to be part of the team sent in to help evacuate approved civilians.

This was the reason I'd joined the army. I wanted to help people. I wanted to do something for my country. I was going to be part of something that counted for more than just meeting a Woolworths 'key performance indicator', like grocery-scanning speed or whatever. This was history. I was going to play a role in it.

The day wore on. There were more briefings, intelligence reports, equipment issues and a lot of waiting around. At lunchtime, I met more of the artillery detachment we would be deploying with: there were about forty soldiers all up. I knew that my job would mainly comprise looking after security issues such as searching people before they got onto the military aircraft and access control of our command base. I hadn't received any formal training on evacuation procedures, and there was no doctrine available about these kinds of operations (or at least none that was made available to me), so I began to pump Murphy for information. What kind of procedures did we follow before allowing civilians onto our aircraft? What was our screening process? How thorough were our searches? What did we do with dangerous or unstable evacuees? What were our rules of engagement?

Murphy did his best to answer my questions but seemed to think I was asking too many. It might sound corny and maybe even ridiculous, but I just wanted to do as professional a job as possible for my corps and my country. I'd gone from having a dead-end job and a lazy boyfriend to a life that involved rescuing people from possible harm. I wanted to be as well prepared as I could.

By mid afternoon, we had deployed to the Amberley RAAF base to await our flight to the base in Butterworth, Malaysia, where we'd run the operation. It was there that the stories of previous failed deployments began to surface. Corporal Monroe recounted how he'd sat at the very same airport, waiting to deploy to PNG for an operation. They'd been sitting on the tarmac, waiting to get on the aircraft, when the deployment was stopped.

I hoped and prayed that this would not happen to us. While we waited, we were given briefings as new information came to hand. At this stage, all forty-odd of us would be deploying to Cambodia to conduct a full-scale service-protected evacuation.

At eight o'clock that night we were still sitting on the tarmac. The C-130 plane scheduled to fly us to Darwin kept being delayed. It was driving me nuts. I just wanted to get on the plane and go. I curled up next to my webbing and tried to get some sleep. I'd only closed my eyes for a few minutes when we were suddenly hustled awake. The Hercules aircraft was about to land.

It was 2 a.m. by the time we arrived in Darwin. We were hurried out of the aircraft and taken to the transit lines for the rest of the night. Murphy and Monroe were still sceptical about our actually getting out of the country, but I remained positive. I gathered up my equipment and headed to our accommodation. They were small rooms, but they were air-conditioned. I slept like a baby.

At 6 a.m. everyone was up for breakfast. We were scheduled to depart for Malaysia at 10 a.m. I feasted on pancakes, Coco Pops and strong coffee – I didn't know when my next decent meal would be. Feeling full and slightly sickened by what I'd eaten, I headed back to my room to pack up my kit. It was there I heard that only twenty personnel from the army contingent would now be going to Cambodia to assist with the evacuation. The rest would remain in Malaysia to help with the processing of the evacuees. Murphy told me that he and I would be the only MPs going to Cambodia.

Ten o'clock came and went. Our kit was put on and taken off the aircraft until the RAAF loadmasters ('loadies') were happy with the weight displacement on the aircraft. At about 1 p.m. the media turned up and their cameras started rolling. Operation VISTA had finally been announced to the Australian public.

The commanders dealt with the media while the rest of us boarded the aircraft. Things were getting exciting again. We were finally on our way. God, it felt good. I savoured the feeling and walked onto the plane with my head held high.

Now, a Hercules aircraft is not like your conventional Qantas jet. There are no comfortable seats, the lighting is limited, and the toilet is hidden only by a flimsy curtain. Everyone sits squashed up together on cargo-netting seats, wearing hearing protection because of the engine noise. That didn't stop me from sleeping the full nine hours it took to get to Malaysia. As soon as we were permitted to remove our seatbelts, I found a vacant bit of real estate and crashed out.

By the time we arrived at Butterworth it was 10 p.m., but the night was not over. There were still intelligence briefings to be given, official passports to be issued and deployment administration to complete. We were also told the news that the detachment would be downsized again. Now only three army personnel would actually deploy to Cambodia the following morning. I didn't know why they kept decreasing the number, but I didn't care too much at the time: I was one of the three selected to go 'into country'.

Although I didn't understand what was happening, I was in no position to air my concerns. I was only a lance corporal. This was a RAAF-led operation and the boss was a wing commander. I just accepted that he was my superior and knew what he was doing. That's how it goes in the defence force. Still, I couldn't comprehend how three army personnel were going to screen, search and contain all the evacuees.

*

The next morning I was up before dawn. I met with the rest of the contingent going into Cambodia: there were medics, loadies, air defence guards, communications personnel and miscellaneous RAAF people. From the army, there was an artillery sergeant and a corporal who'd be accompanying me on the deployment. None of us could wait to get onto the aircraft.

We were standing around, checking our equipment and stores, when we were informed that our numbers had been slashed again. Now only one of us would be deploying. At this stage I had to ask why. It was explained to me that the Cambodian government thought a large-scale army operation would create panic. They wanted a small 'footprint': for all relevant civilians to be evacuated quietly.

So our trio was cut to a solo act. Only one person, from a detachment of forty, would be deploying to Cambodia – and that person would be me. They wanted me because of my security and policing skills, and because I was female. Civilian women and children were our primary concern. Who better to help them through the ordeal than another woman, especially one who could deal with security issues? That day, I thanked my lucky stars for being a woman.

When it was time, I stepped onto the aircraft. I was wide-awake. My senses were alert. The trip would take a couple of hours. I had to relax – calm myself down and enjoy the experience. This was an adventure.

Thirty minutes till landing. I sat watching the clock, wondering how dangerous it would be on the ground. Although there seemed to be little chance of members of the local military acting aggressively towards our detachment, the Cambodian government could not guarantee our safety. We were not permitted to take our rifles into the country, as that was deemed far too antagonistic for an evacuation. I had my army-issued ASP baton concealed under my uniform, but it'd be useless in a firefight. I had complete faith in my commanders – well, perhaps not *complete* faith. I was beginning to understand how big a role publicity plays in operations such as this. In the end, I just accepted that the threat of weapon fire was low.

Two minutes till landing. This was it. Things were about to happen. I had no idea what I was supposed to do once the aircraft landed, but hoped someone in charge would tell me. We touched down. I couldn't see anything as I was stuck in my seatbelt and nowhere near a window. My heart was pounding in my ears. Adrenaline was racing through my body. The rear of the aircraft opened slowly. Whatever I had expected to see, this certainly wasn't it.

Immediately, there was the flashing of cameras. There were reporters and photographers everywhere. There must have been fifty of them, from CNN, ABC – all sorts of agencies. They came scurrying up to the aircraft like mice, pointing microphones, asking questions and shoving cameras in my face.

Fortunately, I was no one of any importance. I knew nothing; I said nothing. I scanned the area after getting off the aircraft. Phnom Penh airport was a train wreck. It had come under heavy fire during the coup, and there were rubble and rubbish littering the severely damaged buildings. There was limited security on the tarmac, as evidenced by the media scrum that now surrounded the aircraft, and no one on the ground who was visibly in command or control. Locals stood around gawking at the hoopla. There was no one around to send them on their way.

I looked around to see what everyone else was doing: loadies were tending to their duties; the air defence guards were trying to clear the tarmac to create a safe environment for the aircraft; other personnel were gathering their equipment. I stood there like a stunned mullet. I had not been given any chain of command to follow. It wasn't clear who, if anyone, I should report to, as I was the only army soldier on the deployment. I knew I had to follow the rank structure within the detachment, but there was no one around to give me specific orders.

It was extremely unsettling: it meant having to find my own place in this operation. I was used to having my orders given to me. In the MPs, I was a lance corporal – at the bottom of the food chain. In this situation, I was the only link in the food chain. It was scary, but also very exciting.

After helping to unload the essential stores from the aircraft, I left for our base – if you could call it that. In fact, it was just a room in the airport. The windows had been blown out and there were glass and detritus everywhere. I looked around the room and checked all the adjoining doors to see if they could open. None did. *Good, only one point of entry to be concerned with.* I saw a group of air defence guards huddled in a circle. I walked over to investigate and heard their commander issuing them a set of orders. I listened in as they were assigned duties around the area. When the orders had been given, I introduced myself to the platoon commander. Together we were able to sort out a list of duties that I could perform in conjunction with his team.

I would be assisting the evacuees to board the aircraft at departure time. I would deal with any distressed civilians and other security issues as they arose. I was happy with that, but there would only be six flights leaving that day. That meant there would also be long periods of non-action in between. We'd have to ensure that the evacuees kept calm while they waited to be flown out.

First things first, though. As a chick in the army, one of my priorities when deploying is always to locate a toilet. Men tend to forget about issues like that, as it's so easy for them to find a wall and just go for it.

I walked out of our base area and into another part of the airport. Pilfering and wanton destruction had left the airport in pretty bad shape. But the toilets were close by. *Yes!* My happiness soon turned sour. There was no power at the airport, so the toilet area was completely dark. I turned on my torch to make sure the ablutions block was empty. There was no bloody way I was going to walk on my own into a dark toilet in an unstable country.

The toilets were empty of people, but full of faeces. It was everywhere. The floor was covered in crap, piss and toilet paper. I gagged as I walked straight out of there and back to the base area. What the hell was I going to do? I was busting! No one else in the detachment really cared about my situation; it was the least of their problems. It was times like this I felt jealous of men.

I grabbed some toilet paper from my ration pack and walked back to the toilets. I'd just have to squat. I held my breath for as long as I could, and then breathed through my mouth so that I couldn't smell the foul stench. I found a relatively unspoilt patch of ground and did my thing. I walked out of the toilet, relieved. I smiled wickedly to myself when I saw two female nurses walk into our base. They didn't know what they were in for.

We were given approximate times for the RAAF aircraft to land and then transport the evacuees out of the country. I went to get a heads-up from the loadies on what their procedures were for getting civilians onto the aircraft and into their seats. They didn't know how things were going to run, but said they'd let me know if they heard anything. No one had any concept of what would happen. This was going to be interesting. I couldn't visualise how we could meet all the security requirements while loading these passengers on board.

Eventually, I was able to get some information from a RAAF officer. He told me that all the passengers would be brought out onto the tarmac, and it would be my job to guide them onto the plane. After getting them into their seats and showing them how to put their seatbelts on, I was then to check passengers' tickets. It was better than not having a plan at all, I supposed, but I wondered whether someone should check the evacuees' tickets before allowing them onto the military aircraft. I aired my concerns but was told that time was of the essence. The pilots did not want to be sitting on the tarmac for very long. They wanted to land, load up and then take off very quickly: a 'turn and burn' operation.

Our first load of passengers was almost due. Would they be scared? Would they act irrationally? I had just had to expect a little bit of everything. There was no known immediate danger to them; we were here to help. This was what the defence force was all about – helping our people. I was where I was supposed to be: here on the front line, giving my all.

A huge number of people waited out on the tarmac: only some of them were the civilians we'd been brought in to evacuate. It was nearing noon and the airport was already crowded. I hoped the approved passengers were carrying their tickets, otherwise it would be impossible to distinguish the authorised evacuees from the would-be stowaways. The officer in charge showed me the type of ticket the approved passengers had to produce once on board.

Checking the tickets after the passengers were on the plane had sounded okay in theory, but, as I'd suspected, it worked like crap. There's a reason tickets are checked prior to people getting on an aircraft. The civilians were led onto the Hercules through its rear opening. I took them to the front end of the plane and checked tickets as I made my way to the rear. The plane was crowded and there was so much going on. The first person I came to had an unauthorised ticket. As I signalled to an air defence guard to escort him off the plane, I could see that there were at least five more people nearby with fake tickets. The situation was ridiculous: I was evicting lots of people from their seats, but there were not enough military personnel to ensure that they were actually taken off the plane. The unauthorised passengers would simply walk two steps away, then sit down in a new seat, hoping I wouldn't notice.

One of them got down on his hands and knees and begged me not to send him off. There was nothing I could do for him. As I attempted to escort him off, he struggled against my grip. He was a small man. My size and strength (and, of course, my pain compliance hold) were enough to overpower him. I called over an air defence guard to make sure he got off. There were still plenty more tickets to be checked. Then I heard someone telling me to hurry up.

Before I knew it, I was being told to leave the plane, as it was about to take off. I couldn't believe it. I told the officer in charge that we'd evicted some unauthorised people, but there were still at least five on board who were not supposed to be there. It was to no avail: the pilots were on a deadline. They had to be off the tarmac.

I was fuming, and I let the officer know it. Well, actually, that's a fib. I told the loadie, who then told the officer, that the tickets needed to be checked prior to letting the passengers onto the aircraft. I thought my advice would be far better coming from him, than from a soldier like me. The loadie had a higher rank than mine, and also an established relationship with the officer. Two hours later we heard that a big deal had been made over the fact that nine unauthorised people had managed to make it to Malaysia. It was no surprise to me.

The next aircraft arrived, and this time the tickets were checked before passengers were allowed onto the aircraft. There were no stowaways on this flight. However, the pilots were still exacting about their timelines. On the fourth aircraft out, I had to jump off the ramp while the plane was taxiing towards the runway. I'd been busy checking seatbelts when I felt the aircraft move: they were bloody well leaving before making sure all relevant personnel were off the craft. So I leapt off the ramp in spectacular fashion while waving all the passengers goodbye.

Later that evening, I was standing on the tarmac with two RAAF blokes. We'd been discussing the latest flight when some Cambodian soldiers drove by. On spotting us, they slowed down, and then their vehicle stopped about 20 metres away. We had been advised that we were under no threat so we weren't too concerned. The soldiers must have been overdosing on testosterone and a sense of self-importance, though, because one of them then pulled out a rocket-propelled grenade (RPG) launcher and pointed it right at us. The three of us stood together, completely vulnerable: out in the open, unarmed. Our closest backup was at least 200 metres away, and no one had any weapons. My ASP baton was tucked in under my shirt, but it'd be pretty bloody useless against an RPG.

The soldier held it in our direction for only a moment before putting it down again. They drove off hurriedly, and we didn't see them again. Did he really think he was a hard man, pointing his weapon at us? What a tosser! RPGs are notorious for discharging accidentally. I shudder to think what might have happened because some foreign soldier had been caught up in a pissing contest.

The final aircraft arrived at about 9 p.m. that night. It was raining. There was still no electricity at the airport, and only a few of us had torches. After escorting all the remaining passengers onto the aircraft and settling them in, I found my seat and sank into it. As we took off, the aircraft began to fill with smoke. Something was up. I looked around the cabin, but no one else seemed too worried. The smoke eventually dissipated. *Hmm, I might have to enquire about that once we land.*

We arrived in Malaysia late that night. I was released from duty shortly after landing, as I wasn't needed for anything else that night. I returned to my quarters, pulled out my sleeping-bag, and crashed.

I woke feeling the sun on my face. It was a lovely morning. After brekkie, my day was filled with briefing commanders, intelligence officers and other members of the detachment on what had occurred in Cambodia. I was told that the white smoke I'd seen on the aircraft was in fact the result of the pilot's releasing flares. The pilot believed that a foreign force had targeted the aircraft and that there was a missile lock on the Hercules. He engaged the anti-missile defence system to release flares, and some residual smoke had entered the aircraft. It wasn't known whether the C-130 had truly been a target or if the pilot was just a little jumpy and acted prematurely. Whatever the explanation, it was going to make my story more interesting.

Later on, after a few beers, I started regaling the others with my glory stories. Instead of my jumping off the RAAF aircraft as it slowly started to roll, the story changed to my commando-rolling off the aircraft as it was lifting off into the air. The story about the tough guy pointing his RPG at us changed to a maniacal super-villain trying to take us prisoner and threatening to blow our brains out. And then there was my great escape on the last flight out of the country: the Cambodians were trying to shoot us down and the pilots were forced to release anti-missile flares so we could escape. All very exciting (and untrue), but what's a war story without a little gloss?

Bruce and I eventually got engaged and, in due course, I became pregnant. I was also selected to undertake officer training at the Royal Military College (RMC) in Canberra. Things were going great, both professionally and personally.

Bruce and I eagerly awaited the arrival of our baby. I was amazed and fascinated at what was going on inside me. I was creating life: a new little person who would come into the world. I couldn't wait to be a mum; Bruce couldn't wait to be a dad. We were going to be the perfect little family.

As the months went by, I no longer fitted into my camouflage army uniform and had to start wearing a maternity dress. I'd expected my stomach to grow, but I was shocked to find it wasn't my only body part that changed. Suddenly I had a huge arse. My ankles swelled up, my face ballooned and ugly stretch marks appeared on my stomach.

I maintained a good fitness program throughout most of my pregnancy, but eventually I had to let it go. I couldn't walk even the short distance between my desk and the office printer without having to take a detour to the toilet. But as soon as I felt my son move inside me, I knew it was all worth it. What was a little discomfort compared to getting to hold a little baby boy in my arms?

I worked right up until I went into labour. Bruce and I had just finished decorating the nursery. I collapsed into bed, and lay there for about ten minutes before I suddenly felt myself gushing liquid. My waters had broken! Straightaway, Bruce and I left for the hospital. Eight hours later our son was born.

Kane – 'son of the warrior'. I was a warrior. Bruce was a warrior. The name was perfect for our son, my gorgeous little boy. I really took to motherhood. Having watched my mother breastfeed Naomi, I was completely comfortable with nursing my son. It was an intimate and special thing we shared: an experience that is hard to put into words. In the hospital bed, I held my baby in my arms, kissed him gingerly on the check and welcomed him into the world.

After that, life became a whirlwind. There were nappies to be washed, feedings at all hours and limited sleep. But it was glorious. It was fulfilling and rewarding, and most of all it was just great fun. My maternity leave was all too short. I took extra leave without pay. That's when things started to get tough financially. We weren't lacking in anything, but I couldn't waste money on clothes and shoes anymore. We had to think of the future.

With great reluctance, I returned to work once my leave was up. It took a while to settle in again. It helped that I set myself a few goals. Determined to get my figure and my fitness back, I embarked on a rigorous training and diet regimen. I had 20 kilograms to lose and a fitness test to pass. With Bruce and my decision to move to Canberra so I could commence my officer training, I had a lot of work to do.

I worked my arse off – literally and metaphorically. I managed to lose the weight, but it was no easy feat. Chicken Twisties and

Cadbury chocolate were my weaknesses. My fitness improved, and soon I was at an acceptable level. I was still no marathon runner (or sprinter, as it happened), but I met the required physical standards and that was what mattered.

At the start of the new millennium, we moved to Canberra so that I could study to become an army officer. I didn't want to give up this chance to become an officer or give up being a mum. Somehow I juggled the two roles. Kane was ten months old when I started at RMC. I weaned him off breastfeeding a week before I started training, and Bruce took over his care during the day. Officer training was intense. It was definitely one of the most challenging times of my life: it was tactics, drill, PT, tactics, field exercises, tactics, defence writing and tactics. The days were long, and the nights longer. By day I was a staff cadet at training college, and by night I was a mum.

I'd escape the rigid training institution and return home to my son. I didn't want Kane to forget who I was. Each night I bathed him, fed him and put him to sleep. As I lay with him to settle him down, I'd often fall asleep from exhaustion, not waking until my alarm went off at four in the morning.

I wanted to spend every spare minute I had with my family, and homework always came last. My alarm was set so I could work on my assignments before Kane woke up. At four in the morning it is hard to focus on the weapon characteristics of an Abrams tank as compared to those of a Leopard tank. No wonder I was struggling through tactics lessons.

Eighteen months later I graduated from the college. My parents had moved back to Newcastle, New South Wales, so they were now living close enough to come to my March Out parade. In July 2001, my father looked on proudly as I received my commissioned rank of lieutenant at our graduation ceremony. To top things off, I was placed ninth on the Queen's Medal ranking for my performance during the whole course. Not bad for a mum, eh?

My relationship with Bruce had been put under considerable strain during my time at RMC, but at last things would go back to normal. After a lot of discussion, we thought it best that I join the medical corps as an administration officer up in Brisbane. It would be a job that allowed for a more stable family life.

In August I attended medical and logistical training in Wagga Wagga, while Bruce organised our move to Brisbane. The plan was that his mum would accompany him on the long drive north, and then I would fly up to meet up him once my course had finished. We'd bought a second-hand SS Commodore just before I left for training, and Bruce was eager to give it a good run. We had been allocated an army house in Brisbane to live in, but couldn't move in straightaway because we had to wait for our furniture to arrive from Canberra. Hotel accommodation was arranged for us to stay in until it arrived.

I couldn't get off the plane at Brisbane fast enough, expecting to see their happy faces at the gate. But Kane's cheery face was all I got. I hugged and kissed him and held him in my arms. He was two and a half years old by now and fantastically adorable. I went to hug and kiss Bruce too, but he was standoffish – distant and quiet. His mother wasn't with him; apparently she was off visiting a friend for the night. I knew something was up. On the drive home, the only conversation I had was with Kane.

I'd been away on the course for just over a month, and during that time Father's Day had come and gone. When we had settled into the hotel room, I gave Bruce the gifts I'd purchased, including a card from Kane and me. He quietly opened the presents, before putting them aside. Kane moved off into his bedroom to play with his toys, and that's when Bruce finally opened up: "I'm leaving. I don't love you anymore." I sat in shocked silence.

I couldn't believe what I was hearing. We had bought a family car the month before. We had looked forward to a better future together. What the hell was going on? "I know things were tough while I was studying, but things are going to be better now. I'll have normal working hours now. I'll be Kane's main carer now. We can focus on *us* now. We are supposed to be getting married," I said. But Bruce just sat there, stony-faced. I kept asking him, "Why? Why are you going?"

All he would say was that he didn't love me anymore. And that fucking hurt. He was being completely honest with me, but that was no consolation. I wanted to know why he no longer loved me. What had I done wrong? I argued that we should work on our problems first before just giving up – we should try for Kane's sake, if nothing else. But Bruce would only say, "I can't make myself love you, if I don't feel that way."

I knew we had grown apart. Our sex life had changed dramatically during my training, and my long hours and weeks away from home did us no favours either. I thought Bruce understood, though: he was a soldier too. Surely he recognised the needs of the army. During my eighteen months at RMC, I had focused most of my attention on Kane. He was a baby. He needed his mother. I thought Bruce could handle it, but I was wrong. I guess he needed me too.

Bruce had decided he needed to go his own way. He was happy with his decision. It was a big relief for him to finally come out and say it. But I was devastated – completely and utterly devastated. We were going to get married. We were going to make a new life together. It was all disappearing before my eyes. And, to top things off, I had to march into my new unit the very next morning.

I awoke the following day with a splitting headache. I didn't want to face the world. My life was in tatters. Bruce, the man I thought I would grow old with, had dumped me. I was suddenly a single parent in a new town, and I didn't know how I was going to handle it. Our furniture was due to arrive in a few days' time, but now only Kane and I would be moving into the house. Bruce made arrangements to live in the soldier accommodation on base and sorted out Kane's enrolment in day care. Everything was organised and planned from his perspective, but emotionally, I was a wreck.

And now I had to report for duty. I had to put on a mask and pretend that everything was okay. Even before Bruce dropped the bombshell, I had been nervous about my first day as a lieutenant. I'd been a soldier for eight years. Officers were smart. Officers were leaders. Officers always knew what to do. Now I was one of them.

I dropped Kane off at day care, reported for duty, did my job, and then came home. That became my life: work, look after Kane, work, sleep. Shortly after Bruce walked out of my life, I realised I didn't want to be in medical corps. We had discussed my going back into the MP when I was at RMC, but dismissed it, as it hadn't fitted in with our 'family plans'. Everything had changed now. I wanted to be in the MP again. I applied for a corps transfer, knowing that it could take years to be processed.

For the next year and a half, I struggled along. Bruce was hardly ever in Brisbane as he was either deployed on operations or attending courses. He'd see Kane on the occasional weekend and talk to him on the phone, but, for the most part, it was just my son and me. I had no life outside of Kane. I wasn't interested in going out and meeting anyone new. I wanted to concentrate on my son and make things the best I could for him. I always stayed upbeat around him. My pain was my own – just because I was hurting, didn't mean that he should have to hurt too.

In January 2003, my transfer was finally accepted, and I started work as the platoon commander of the Brisbane-based MP platoon. I would be responsible for thirty soldiers. In medical corps, I had mostly dealt with administration, logistical and training issues. Now it'd be up to me to command my soldiers, plan security missions, complete policing tasks, and oversee soldier welfare and training. It was scary, but I was definitely up for the challenge.

Major Murray Heron, who had been my platoon commander back in my early days in the corps, was now my company commander. He was a good leader, and someone who I had the utmost respect for. Major Heron was the kind of boss who'd give you a task, tell you what the parameters were, let you formulate your plan, and, if needed, ask you to justify a particular course of action. He'd draw you into line if it was required, and provide guidance and support to bring out your best. There was no one else I would have rather worked under.

The training warrant officer at the unit was none other than Leo Legend, my instructor from my MP basic course. Leo had always inspired me to work to a standard I'd thought to be unreachable. His style of leadership was motivating, confident and fair.

I was also lucky that my platoon sergeant major (or second-in-command) was Craig, another instructor from my course. Craig was the strong, silent type who provided me with oodles of solid advice from his many years with the MP. He was my counsellor and my sounding board. Being a leader can be a lonely job because you are required to make decisions that may not be popular. If you find yourself being too familiar with staff, it can sometimes affect the outcome of important decisions. A certain amount of aloofness is required, so that your decisions are unbiased and are made responsibly. This is an important aspect of leadership as it prevents strong personalities or 'boys clubs' from influencing people in power. It creates equity in the workplace and allows the leader to make the right decision without being swayed by their 'friends'. I never realised just how important this was, until I saw it flagrantly ignored years later. So Craig was a very important person to me. It was vital to have a second-in-command who I could trust implicitly, to discuss work, staffing and personal issues with.

One of the sergeants under my command, Clappy, was a guy who I had served alongside when I was a soldier. In fact, he had been in charge of me back then. I was now his boss. Things were not as awkward as they might have been. I'd assign him tasks, and it would be up to him how to do them. If he did them well, I told him so. If he stuffed up (which he never did, just for the record), he'd get extra training. It was how things worked with everyone in my platoon.

I don't know if I was a good leader or not, but I will say this: I ran my platoon as best I could. When I assigned my soldiers a task, I expected them to complete the job competently. If I had to plan a mission, I'd take my own knowledge on the matter and combine it with advice from my sergeants. If soldiers or platoon sergeants were crap at their jobs, I counselled them and took steps to remedy the problem. With my platoon, I knew I had complete loyalty, and that was what counted the most. In return, they had my unwavering loyalty too.

While in the unit, I was given the opportunity to try out for the elite MP close personal protection (CPP) course. Only one or two officers were permitted to attend the course at a time, as most of the positions were given to the corporals. Selection to attend the course was only the first hurdle I had to jump over. I then had to pass the 'barrier test' before I could even start the course. The barrier test was designed to weed out candidates who aren't physically ready for the demands of the course. The barrier test included push-ups, sit-ups, a timed 2.4-kilometre run followed by a 'beep test' (a shuttle run), a swim test and a weapons shoot. The pass standard was bloody high, and well above normal military fitness requirements. Now, if you can recall my previous stories about not being a fast runner and a natural athlete, then you can probably appreciate the considerable amount of effort I put into passing that test.

The training paid off. I kicked arse on the barrier test and went on to complete the course, which was even more gruelling. It involved five weeks of intensive training, and every minute of it was thrilling. I loved conducting reconnaissance missions late into the night. I loved practising our 'walking drills' on the busy streets of Sydney. My lower back and knee were pretty well stuffed for most of the course thanks to over-training, but when enemy fire started raining down on us during battle simulations, the adrenaline kicked in and any thoughts of pain went out the window. I ducked, weaved and returned fire with the rest of the team. It was the best course I'd ever done: it was physically demanding, mentally draining, but a hell of a lot of fun! I was ecstatic when I learnt I had passed the course. I had worked hard and was extremely proud to be the first female officer qualified to command CPP teams on military operations.

As a female leader in the army, I found that I had to be above average in all areas of the job in order to be thought of as equal to my male counterparts. The army was filled with fit, strong, testosterone-fuelled men, and I needed to be 'special' in order to be accepted into their realm. All women did. It wasn't a rule or obligation; it was just something that you did to gain credibility as a leader, in a male-dominated workplace. Completing the CPP course bolstered my reputation as a female leader, and I hoped it would propel my career within the MP.

My career might have been red-hot, but I still had no personal life to speak of. When Bruce first told me there was someone new in his life, I was hurt. He wanted to introduce me to his new wife, Pamela, but even the thought of it was too much. It didn't help that she was a stunning blonde with a top executive job – she was basically everything I wasn't. I didn't want to meet her. I didn't want to sit down and have a cup of coffee with her, and I certainly didn't want to imagine her anywhere near my son. Bruce didn't respond well either, and things turned bitter on both sides. I wasn't sure why I was still so upset about breaking up with Bruce after almost two years of being apart. I didn't love him anymore and I wasn't pining after him. I just wasn't healing.

As my relationship with Bruce continued to deteriorate, work went off the rails. My soldiers and sergeants were being deployed on operations, and I found myself left with an understaffed platoon for most of the year. At one stage there was only me and fifteen soldiers – half the size the platoon should have been – which meant a big increase in my work, as I had no sergeants to share the load.

At first I relished all these challenges, but after twelve high-tempo months it just got plain hard. Even the Christmas period did nothing to help my exhaustion. By the time I returned to work, I was well and truly burnt out.

I started 2004 feeling despondent and unmotivated. I loved my job, but I was tired. Being a single mum was tough. All too often I found myself driving Kane to my mum's house at the weekend (a twenty-hour round trip), so I could attend mandatory army field exercises. I'd then have to repeat that trip the following weekend to pick him up. I loved the training exercises, but the travel was tough on Kane; it was also tough on me.

I had got so much from being a soldier and an officer. Joining up all those years ago was the best decision I ever made, but things had changed. At work, I wanted to invest all my time and effort in my job. I wanted to plan missions, attend exercises and be the best leader I could. When I was at home, I wanted to immerse myself in Kane's life. I wanted to bake cupcakes, attend playgroups and socialise with other mothers. As things stood, I wasn't doing either to my satisfaction: my mind was always in two places.

I also had a deep sense that I wanted something more out of life. I wanted an adventure. I had spent the past three years just reacting to whatever situation came my way, and it was starting to wear on me. What sort of example was I setting for my son? I needed to show him the benefits of being bold, of making your own opportunities rather than just waiting for them to be handed to you.

So I began to think about other options. I'd heard about the emerging security contractor scene in Iraq. What was the good of having all these skills if I couldn't put them to use? My whole adult life I'd trained to work in a war zone, and yet I couldn't do so as a female officer. But, in the security sector, the possibilities were limitless. It was far from an easy decision. I wrestled with how it would affect my son, and ruminated torturously on the 'what if' scenarios. How would Kane cope without me for six months – the length of the typical contract? What if something happened to me while I was over there? These were difficult, soul-searching questions. I thought of the fathers I knew who took up these sorts of contracts all the time without a second thought. After lengthy discussions with Bruce, in which he suggested that Kane could stay with him while I was away working, it looked as though it might be feasible. I still agonised over leaving my son but, in the end, I decided it was better to show Kane that it paid to take life by the balls. Apprehensively, I resigned from the army.

I made some enquiries and, before I knew it, I had a job lined up as part of a private security detail (PSD). Kane would live with his dad for the six months I'd be away, and when I returned on leave (I would have a month's holidays halfway through the contract), I would be a stay-at-home mum. This was a life-changing decision, and making it felt electric.

On a beautiful summer's day in early November 2004, Kane and I travelled to Canberra, where Bruce and Pamela were living. My connecting flight out of the country was due to leave that evening.

Kane and I hung out together all day, doing whatever he wanted. We went to the movies, mucked around at KidCity – a huge indoor play centre – and ate ice-cream until our stomachs hurt. I'd see Kane with this huge smile on his face, and I had to fight to keep myself together. Kane was everything to me. God knows it broke my heart to leave him, but I knew how much Bruce was looking forward to spending this time with his son. I was certain Kane would get a lot out of this time with his dad too.

At the end of the day, I dropped off Kane at his father's place. I hugged him long and hard, promising that I would write to him and ring as often as I could. I passed Kane over to Bruce, knowing he would be well taken care of. Fighting back the tears, I told my son how much I loved him and that I'd be home again before he knew it. It was more than I could bear. After a last hug I turned and left.

I numbly drove back to the airport hotel, where I had a long, hot shower. It was there that I let it all out. I broke down and wept for my son. Eventually, I stepped out of the shower feeling drained but somewhat at peace. I had made my decision, and I was not going to change my mind. Despite the sadness of leaving my little boy, I felt a tingle as I dried myself with the fluffy white towel. I was excited to find out what was waiting for me outside Baghdad airport.

I changed into my cargo pants and thick, black army boots. There'd be no more pretty-girl clothes for me. I grabbed my belongings and had one more look around my room. There was no turning back now. I shut the door behind me and left for the airport.

After three days in transit, and more connections and palm greasing than I care to mention, I was in a plane above Baghdad. It was clear things were done differently here. There was no gentle descent towards the runway followed by a smooth landing. Thanks to the ever-present threat of surface-to-air missiles, the pilot had to fly in tight circles, staying in the 'safe' airspace, gradually getting lower and lower to the ground. Then the aircraft seemed to just drop onto the tarmac with a thud. It was a unique experience, but one that left me a little nauseated.

After we'd clunked onto the ground, there was a mad rush to get off the plane. The etiquette didn't seem to include waiting for the person in front to get off first. So I followed suit, pushing my way into the aisle and off the plane. My fellow passengers and I travelled in a decrepit-looking bus across the tarmac to the passport office.

The passport office had only the most basic of facilities. There were four cubicles for passport and visa checking, but only two of them were manned. Foreign security guards, dressed in protective equipment and armed to the teeth, were everywhere. I began to wonder exactly how dangerous the airport was. But, at that moment, actually getting to see any other part of the airport was my first big obstacle.

I didn't have a visa to enter Iraq. I had been advised that all I needed to do was flash the officials the front page of my security contract, and then they would let me in without question. No dice. In the end, it came down to money. The man with the stamp wanted some, and I had it. After paying him US$50, I was let in.

I picked up my luggage from a broken-down conveyor belt, and headed over to customs – and by 'customs', I mean a man sitting behind a small table. I took out my knives, weapon holsters, chest webbing and other war-time toys, but my kit barely roused the man's interest; he simply waved me through. I walked out the door, scanning for anyone who might be waiting for me. I noticed a tall, skinny man striding my way.

"G'day, Joycee. How are ya?" the beanpole said, leaning over to give me a quick kiss on the cheek. I hesitated slightly until I realised that it was Merlin, an MP mate from way back. I hardly recognised him. It had been about ten years since I'd seen him, and he'd grown a beard in the meantime.

"Mate, what are you doing here?" I asked, as he grabbed one of my bags. Merlin told me he was working as security advance team (SAT) leader for our company. I gave a sigh of relief: I'd know someone on the team – someone well qualified, to boot. Merlin had been a corporal in the army before he got out to work in PNG as a security contractor. He had also done the MP CPP course.

As we walked over to the car park, I asked him about the security situation at the airport. Merlin explained that the area was relatively safe because of its proximity to a huge American base called Camp Victory, which was where we'd be going next. Some of the guys on the team, who were waiting for us by the vehicles, were keen to pick up some supplies. The Green Zone, also known as the International Zone, was a highly fortified area within Baghdad city where our team lived. Everywhere outside the Green Zone and the Camp Victory–airport area was referred to as the Red Zone, and as the name suggests, it was extremely dangerous out there. It had a post exchange (PX) store but it was nothing compared to the one the Americans had. The Camp Victory PX sold a good range of food, clothing and DVDs. It even had a Burger King.

Merlin warned that while this area might be safe, the road we'd need to take to get to the Green Zone was not. Route Irish was known as the BIAP Road, or the Jihad Road to the locals. It was one of the most dangerous roads in the world: many, many people had been killed on it. The 12-kilometre highway was the only route to the airport. As such, both military personnel and civilians often used it, making it a popular target for insurgent attacks.

The insurgents' tactics varied. Suicide bombers would sometimes drive alongside their target's car before detonating their explosives. Other times they would stand at the side of the road with their car bonnet raised to give the impression that they'd broken down, waiting for a convoy of security vehicles to pass before they pressed the button. Or the crafty pricks would plant explosives inside dead animals and place them next to the road. They'd drop grenades from overpasses, shoot rocket-propelled grenades and guns from nearby building windows, and set up banks of claymore mines, once again hoping to take out whoever they could. They were indiscriminate in who they targeted: military and security personnel, civilians and locals; they didn't care as long as the body count kept rising. How do you reason with a bunch of arseholes who don't even respect their own people, let alone a foreign military force?

Merlin took me to the undercover car park, where I met the rest of the team. The introductions were kept very brief. I noticed that they wore all their tactical kit with large shirts over the top to obscure it. Some had grown beards and were wearing Arabic scarves, known as 'shemaghs', around their heads.

A guy named Ghost introduced himself while handing me a Glock pistol. I attached it to my belt. Next, he gave me an AK-47. *What a bloody archaic weapon*, I thought. I wondered where my M-4 was: my contract from the security company had indicated that it was the team's weapon of choice. An M-4 has a higher rate of fire, and is more accurate and a lot easier to use than the dinosaur I was currently holding. Ghost must have noticed my raised eyebrows. He told me that the company had not been able to get any M-4s into the country as yet, and that they were using AK-47s in the meantime.

I'd never used one before, but I'd heard its operation was fairly easy to pick up. The AK's bullet calibre was larger than an M-4's, so if I had to use it, at least it would leave the target with some damage. If I had to shoot an insurgent to protect myself and the team, then I wanted to do it effectively. The AK-47 was certainly up to the job.

After I was kitted up with weapons, body armour and ammunition, we drove the short distance to Camp Victory. Ghost told me to bat my eyelids at all the checkpoint guards, as I was the only team member without the ID card needed to get into the base. As it turned out, I was able to slip in along with the team, and soon I was stuffing my face with Burger King.

While the other guys went off to buy their supplies, Ghost stayed to keep me company. We had a getting-to-know-you chat:

he told me he had a thirteen-year-old son whose mother he'd split from many years ago. He'd recently knocked up another woman, but wasn't sure if he wanted to be with her either. I asked him about his previous experience, and he explained that he had been a medic in the British army. He'd been attached to the parachute battalion, which I took to mean that he'd worked with a combat unit, but he was a trade-qualified medic.

Ghost went on to say that he was the team medic as well as the counter assault team (CAT) leader. Now I was confused. The role of the CAT is to go in and shoot the shit out of the enemy when the team is under attack. It provides massive fire support so the rest of the team and the client can withdraw somewhere safer. I didn't understand how someone could be a life preserver at the same time as leading an attack team. Tactically, it was just plain wrong. Moreover, a CAT leader should have considerable tactical knowledge and skills. Ideally, it's a job for an ex–special forces soldier or, at a pinch, an infantry corporal with a shitload of experience. But a medic? I was sceptical to say the least.

I took a deep breath in. It was way too early to make any judgments. Anyhow, I knew firsthand what it was like to be underestimated. As a woman in this industry, I would have to fight hard to be taken seriously. I was now in a man's world, and that meant proving I was as capable as, if not better than, my male teammates.

I was no longer an officer in the army. There was no more planning war games, delivering orders or leading my soldiers. I was just a security contractor, paid to follow orders and do my job. And that was what I was going to do.

It's a shame I couldn't stick to that plan and keep my mouth shut. It would have saved me a lot of heartache. But shit happens and you find yourself unable to keep quiet any longer. And when you break the silence, all hell breaks loose with it.

The time came to leave the safety of Camp Victory and head into the unknown. I lifted my body armour up over my head and onto my shoulders. Heavy and thick, it extended down to the top of my thighs. I tightened the straps around my waist, and adjusted my pistol so that it was within easy grasp. I grabbed my AK-47, hoping that it was zeroed, and loaded a magazine full of rounds onto it. A zeroed weapon is one that has been test-fired to ensure that the bullet goes where you want it to. It can mean the difference between life and death in a hostile environment.

I was given a run-down of our strategy for getting back to the Green Zone: we'd be driving down Route Irish as fast as we could, trying not to get hit. Funny, yes, but I was interested in the actual plan, which no one in the team seemed to want to share. As far as they were concerned, they were providing me with an armed escort back to the Green Zone, treating me as if I were a client they were hired to protect.

I was happy enough with that idea, even though it perplexed me why they wouldn't want to use me as an extra shooter. I made the best of it and decided to use the trip to take a good look at the situation I was heading into. I would be able to observe topography, roads, bridges, people and other cars on the roads. It would also allow me to observe how my team operated in this environment and the tactics they employed.

I climbed into the back seat of the 'client vehicle' and instantly realised it was not armoured. In fact, none of the vehicles was armoured. The first vehicle, known as the 'advance team', was a ten-year-old BMW car. The second vehicle, the client car, was also an old BMW. The third vehicle, which carried the CAT, was a wagon.

These cars wouldn't protect those inside them from a rock let alone a bullet or a rocket-propelled grenade. This was going to be a game of chance, with the prize being arriving in the Green Zone alive. *Bugger their idea of treating me like a client.* I wanted more ammo before I was going anywhere. One magazine was just not enough!

The driver of my vehicle was a guy named Baloo. He was an ex–British royal marine who had close personal protection experience. I asked him if there were any more AK magazines. He couldn't believe I had only been given the one.

"You'll need these more than I will," Baloo said, throwing his backpack my way. Inside were about ten full magazines. "If we get into trouble, you'll need to open fire on the enemy so that I can concentrate on driving." It was the best plan I'd heard so far. I sat in the back seat and set myself up for the trip down Route Irish. My ammo was within easy reach for quick magazine changes, and I held my AK at the ready.

I sat directly behind Baloo so that I could scan the road to his left and to the rear of our left-hand-drive vehicle. I didn't know much about the guy in the front passenger seat, but I knew he would be scanning the front and right-hand side of the vehicle. All in all, we had a 360-degree view around our vehicle.

Baloo turned over the engine, and we started out, passing through a number of military checkpoints. I could see there was only one more between us and Route Irish. The call came over the radio for everyone to "make their weapons ready". I cocked my AK and placed my thumb on the safety catch. If we were attacked, all I would have to do was release the safety and let the bullets fly.

I wiped the sweat from my forehead, gritted my teeth and lightly brushed the cross – a gift from my mother – that I wore around my neck. This was it. We moved through the final checkpoint, and then we were off. Large concrete walls flanked the road, but they were only there to protect the checkpoint area. In a matter of metres, there were no more walls: we were out in the open.

I noticed that the advance vehicle was way out in front of us, and the CAT vehicle way behind. Effectively, there was no protection for our vehicle – the client vehicle. This went against everything I had learnt about close protection. If we were attacked, neither vehicle would be close enough to provide blocking drills to protect us. Maybe they were running this way because I was not a 'real client'? Maybe the strategy was different because we were in soft-skinned vehicles and not armoured ones? Maybe this was just how it was done in Iraq?

As we raced along Route Irish we passed open fields and then old square buildings, which sat on either side of the double-lane highway. The buildings were about 200 metres from the road, and looked to be an excellent place for an insurgent to take a pot shot at us. The traffic was light so we were able to weave in and out of it with little problems. As we passed cars, I glanced inside. There were old men driving alone. There were families of six squashed in all together. Some women wore headscarves; others were dressed in black robes that covered everything apart from a small window showing their eyes. The men wore shirts I suspected had been unloved since the seventies, and the children looked no different to any kid back home. Not many wore what I thought of as traditional Arabic garb. These were just normal people going about their lives.

We continued to tear-arse along the road. As we got closer to the Green Zone, the buildings seemed to close in on us. Along this stretch, the buildings were about 20 metres from the road. I searched for snipers on rooftops or anyone peering out of a window. Traffic grew denser and vehicles began to drive closer to us. I scanned vehicles more intently now, looking for weapons or any suspicious behaviour from passengers.

As we neared the first overpass, I heard the call that the bridge was clear. I knew that meant there was no obvious sign of anyone hanging around, waiting to drop a grenade on us from above. After going through the underpass, Baloo began to slow down. We were approaching the Green Zone checkpoint.

Our car eased closer to the checkpoint. With some of the team wearing their shemaghs, it was easy for the soldiers to mistake them for locals, Baloo said. If we approached the checkpoint too quickly, or before we'd been waved forwards by the soldiers, we risked being shot at by friendly forces. So we pulled up with care, eyeing the other vehicles around us. I hoped desperately that no one was feeling like blowing themselves up that day.

We made it through the checkpoint and into the Green Zone. Baloo visibly relaxed: his shoulders dropping and his frown lines easing. The zone's perimeter was lined with huge concrete walls, and there were gun posts set up at regular intervals around the boundary. The greatest threat to those within the Green Zone came from mortar attacks, where insurgents fired rockets from outside the perimeter. On the occasions the insurgents managed to get a few rounds inside, the US military were quick to react, sending out a counter-strike force to deal with them.

After turning off onto a dirt road and driving around some back streets, Baloo pulled up outside a large two-storey building. This was our team house.

As I helped to unpack the equipment from the cars, I took a good look around. There were guards stationed at the top of our street. They were locals hired by the company that had its headquarters across the road from us. There was also a guard stationed outside our house. He didn't look that impressive, though. I thought he might be more of an early-warning device than anything else. I said hello to him, and then walked into the front yard of our house.

I didn't know what the rules were for carrying weapons around the house but it seemed polite to unload my AK before I went inside. There were no unloading bays that I could see, so I did my drills in the garden, pointing my weapon at the ground. Bays are used in military environments to provide a safe area for unloading your weapon. If you accidentally discharge your weapon while unloading it, the bullet hits the bay, and not, say, your mate.

I soon found out that there were no rules about carrying loaded weapons indoors; people just did whatever they wanted. They could walk into the house with their weapons at the ready, and keep them that way. Or they could unload them in their bedroom if they chose to. What a change from the army! Despite the lack of weapon-status rules, I was warned that if I fired an 'unauthorised' shot, I'd be sacked on the spot and sent home.

After twelve years in the military without any unauthorised

discharges, I would make damn sure there wasn't a black mark next to my name as a civilian. After carefully clearing my weapon, I headed into the house with all my kit. Ghost took me to my room, which was on the second floor. To get to it, we had to pick our way through a large bedroom that housed five guys. My room was small, and set up with two single beds, but I would have it to myself. I was happy to have my own space, but not impressed that I'd have to walk through a room full of guys in order to get there. I could see all sorts of problems arising.

As well as the beds, the room had two double-sized cupboards – plenty of room for my clothes and equipment. Several old Arabic rugs lined the cement floor, providing some protection from the cold. Iraq was heading into winter, and the mornings and evening were already chilly. An air-conditioner, with dodgy electrical wiring protruding at all angles, was mounted on the wall.

It was getting dark and I was exhausted. All the excitement and jet lag were catching up to me. Ghost told me to relax and get an early night: I wasn't needed for anything more that evening, and I would begin my induction into the team the next day. After chatting for a short while with other team members, I made my excuses and went to bed. I thought of Kane as I pulled back the covers but was asleep within seconds of my head touching the pillow.

I awoke early the next morning, feeling refreshed. I dressed quickly and sneaked out through the guys' room, trying not to disturb anyone. I crept down the stairs and into the kitchen. I noted the basic cooking facilities, but what I was really after was a hot cup of coffee.

I turned on the coffee pot and heated up a fresh brew of strong coffee. This was just what I needed. I grabbed my mug and wandered into the large lounge area. There was a huge television in the corner and maps and important-looking documents hanging on the noticeboards. As I sipped my coffee and read the tidbits of information on the boards, I could hear stirring from the floor above.

The aroma of fresh coffee had wafted throughout the house, and a bunch of bleary-looking men came stumbling into the lounge room, searching for the source of the delicious smell. After pouring several more cups of coffee, I smiled to myself. Today was the start of my new career. I was a member of the security team hired to protect the nine Iraqi electoral commissioners.

That morning, Ghost gave me some background information on our clients. The nine members of the Independent Electoral Commission of Iraq were responsible for organising and promoting the country's first democratic election since Saddam Hussein had been forced from power in 2003. The elections were due to take place in January 2005. According to the US grading system that ranked the threat level posed to high-profile citizens, the commissioners were 'tier one' targets, alongside principal military officers, members of government and other political leaders. Some of the commissioners had even had a fatwa placed on them, meaning Islamic extremists had issued a religious decree that they be killed. So, our clients were right at the top on the insurgents' hit list – I had wanted a challenge and here one was. There was a good reason security contractors were paid so well.

I was told that the plan for that day was for some of the team to conduct security picquets at the clients' workplace, the Convention Center. Meanwhile, a member of the team, Money Shot, would show me around the Green Zone and organise my identification passes.

Before we left, I ducked to the loo. The downstairs toilet was a lot grubbier than the one on my floor, I noted. The toilet seat was also missing, and from Ghost's response when I asked him about it later, it was clear no replacement was due in the near future. Believe it or not, the guys in the team actually complained about the lack of a toilet seat more than I did. God knows how they would have handled things if they'd had to sit down every time they went.

Ghost had warned me that the local sewerage system was crap (yes, a pun), and that the plumbing just couldn't cope with soggy clumps of toilet paper. Everyone had to discard the used paper in a nearby bucket, rather than in the actual toilet system. The cleaners were charged with the wonderful job of disposing of the bucket's contents every day. I felt for them.

The waste didn't, or perhaps couldn't, travel through the underground pipes to get to the sewers. So, every third day, a 'poo truck' would turn up at the house to siphon out all the sewerage. You could always smell the truck coming before you saw it, I was told. Ghost had laughed as he said that the stench of faecal matter would soon become a part of daily life, along with the acrid tang of diesel fumes from the running generators.

After I flushed the toilet, I watched in horror as the water began to rise until it was almost level with the bowl. There it remained for about thirty seconds, before finally receding back down the pipes. I let out a sigh of relief. It appeared that the sewerage system was close to capacity. *It must be poo truck day*, I thought.

I washed my hands in the sink, only to discover that the pipes did not reach all the way to the ground. Water splashed over my boots and onto the floor, before slowly dribbling down the drain. *What a mess!* While I was looking around for a mop, Ghost came over and began to chuckle: "Oh, yeah, don't use that sink. It needs fixing."

Money Shot, a tall, lanky man in his late thirties, stalked out of the team office, ready to take me on my excursion. I asked him what type of equipment we needed, and my tour guide replied that we'd be fine with only our pistols. There were so many military and civilian security personnel in the Green Zone that high-powered rifles weren't required. Pistols tucked in under our shirts, we jumped into one of the team cars and headed off.

Money Shot drove us to the infamous Victory Arch: two sets of huge bronze hands holding crossed swords. This was where Saddam had held ceremonial parades with his army. We idled near the entrance, and I could see helmets cemented into the plinths on which the bronze hands rested. The helmets – 2500-odd on each of the four plinths, so Money Shot said – had belonged to fallen Iranian soldiers killed in the First Persian Gulf War.

The parade ground was so wide and so long that the team regularly used it as somewhere to practise their formation driving, blocking drills, handbrake turns and reverse 180-degree turns. It was the best and probably the only place you could practise high-speed driving in the Green Zone, but I was new to the country and extremely suspicious: it would be the perfect place to sit and gather intelligence.

If I was hired to assassinate someone, the first thing I would do is study their security team. Training in an open and public area, such as the Victory Arch, would make the job easy. Having observed the team's training and reaction to attack drills, I'd be able to come up with a counter plan. I didn't know what the chances were of an insurgent actually breaching the Green Zone's perimeter. Less than a month before I'd arrived, the marketplace had been blown up – killing one person and injuring five others – so it was not impossible.

We drove past the military hospital and the US Embassy – housed in one of Saddam's old palaces – on our way to the gym and PX store. This was the hub of Green Zone life. We walked into the gymnasium and my jaw dropped. There were treadmills, cross trainers, weights and stretching rooms. Large gleaming mirrors lined the walls and there were refrigerators stocked with bottled water for patrons. There were clean, fresh sweat towels everywhere and a sound system pumped electronic music. The gym was as good as any back home. The only ID I'd need to get into the gym was a passport or a US Department of Defense (DOD) card. Here was somewhere I could run: it would be a great stress reliever.

The PX store was small, but had all the essential items: toiletries, magazines, washing powder, combat equipment and clothing. It also sold sweets and chocolates, but if you didn't make it to the store on the day they were put on the shelf, you missed out. Talk about the quick and the hungry.

The next and most important part of the tour was the Baghdad Convention Center and the Al Rasheed Hotel, which were located on opposite sides of the same street. We had to pass through numerous security checkpoints before being allowed to enter the hotel car park. From there, we walked to the Convention Center.

The Convention Center was where our clients worked but in order for me to access it, I'd need an identification (ID) pass. I quickly learnt that life as a security contractor was all about ID passes: the more you had, the higher your status. The power of the ID pass was immense: it dictated your ability to do your job, provided greater access to the military services that made life easier, and could even determine your employability.

A DOD card was the golden ticket. It allowed you tasty American military meals, you could use their top-of-the-line gym and recreation facilities and, most importantly, it ensured priority access through security checkpoints. No DOD pass meant you had to line up at checkpoints with the plebs, which left you at greater risk of being blown up or shot at by insurgent forces.

I didn't have a DOD card, but the rest of the team did. They had stopped issuing those cards to our team once they realised that our contract did not fall under the auspices of the Department of Defense. The guys still retained their cards, but I would have to make do with my passport. The ID card I was after now was the Convention Center (CC) card, which would allow me free access to both the Convention Center and the Al Rasheed Hotel.

Although it was easy enough to get the CC card, it was more difficult to secure its 'extra benefits'. These privileges included being able to escort visitors into the complex and being permitted to drive a vehicle right up to the entrance of the building. The ability to drive a client right up to the front of the building made for a far more secure drop-off and ensured the team looked very professional. Without this access, we'd have to park in the general car park, and schlep our clients the 300 metres to their workplace.

Money Shot led the way to the badging office. There, he spoke to an imposing six-foot-four American army officer who was not keen on giving away 'special access' too easily. Money Shot used all his charm and wit to persuade the officer to change his mind. Eventually, Captain America relented, and I was given my CC card with full privileges.

I placed my card into my ID cardholder. In the Green Zone, you had to have your identification on display at all time. Without it, you risked being arrested by the military police and detained until you could prove who you were – not a fun way to spend an afternoon. I hung my ID cardholder around my neck like a medal and followed Money Shot to the hotel.

It was way past lunchtime and I was starving. After passing through yet more security checkpoints and unloading our pistols, at last we made it into the Al Rasheed Hotel. It housed mostly UN personnel who were all working towards the same thing as our clients: a safe and fair election. I was told they were only occupying certain floors of that building. The higher the floor, the greater the chance it had of being severely damaged in a mortar attack.

We weren't there to talk to the UN personnel. The Al Rasheed Hotel had a military food hall, and our CC cards gave us access to it. I could not believe what I saw when I entered the hall. There were tables laden with breakfast cereals, fruits and snack bars. The fridges were filled with soft drinks, flavoured milk, juices and bottles of water. There was a sandwich bar, a salad bar and a fast-food bar. I didn't know where to go first. Australian mess facilities just didn't compare to this. I could see myself enjoying work if lunch was like this every day.

The next morning, my first working with the clients, gave me a sense of how day-to-day business ran. Our team was responsible for picking up the commissioners at their homes and transporting them to their office in the Convention Center. Sometimes our clients coordinated their start timings so that we were able to give them all a lift into work at once. But all too often, they didn't match up and we'd end up making numerous trips to pick them up. Several clients were staying in temporary digs out in the Red Zone while they waited for their Green Zone accommodation to be refurbished. They were in no hurry to move, as they didn't believe they were in any serious danger. I wish I could have felt the same certainty. Thankfully, the team was only contracted to pick up those clients living in the Green Zone, which at the time, was two out of the nine of them.

After accompanying the commissioners to their office, team members sat at a nearby security desk so that, if anything happened, they could respond quickly. If the clients had to go anywhere – for meetings, even just out for lunch – they had to have an escort. At any one time, there were four team members rostered on to look after the clients. Two team members would man the desk, while the other two had a 'rest'. It was one hour on, one hour off. I was assured this made for long and boring days. There were a couple of computer ports near the desk so, if the guys brought their laptops, they could at least access the internet. At the end of each day, the team was responsible for driving the clients back home.

Our team's procedures dictated that two vehicles must always be used when transporting a client. One vehicle carried a driver, a bodyguard and the client, and the other, used as the security vehicle, was occupied by a driver and a shooter. Those in the security vehicle would watch for any suspicious activity and provide extra manpower should any shit go down. The threat in the Green Zone was deemed to be low, so there were no advance vehicles or CAT vehicles involved in these pick-ups. As only four people were out on security picquet at any time, those who weren't rostered for duty with the clients stayed at the team house and trained, watched movies, took care of personal admin or, if there were team members or clients to pick up or drop off at Baghdad airport, went on BIAP runs.

I couldn't help but think about what I would do differently if I were commanding my own team. If I'd had more resources available on my team than the two vehicles and four client escorts, then I would have used them. We picked up the clients in full combat uniform. We wore armoured vests, brought large amounts of ammunition in our chest webbing and carried our rifles. If the threat was high enough that we came prepared for a major firefight, surely it was high enough to justify using a full team.

But I was still thinking as an officer, not as a contractor. I reasoned that I wasn't privy to the sort of threat analysis or intelligence reports that others on the team were. The team leaders had been in Baghdad for a long time; surely they knew what they were doing.

*

For my first client pick-up I was designated the position of driver, luckily behind the wheel of the security vehicle, not the client vehicle. Baloo was stuck being the client's driver. No one liked that job. As the client's driver, you had to be so careful and responsible. There was no sharp braking or cool tactical driving, only changing gears as smoothly as possible and making gentle turns.

There were plenty of speed humps in the Green Zone – and when I say speed humps, I should really say 'speed mountains'. They were huge, designed to slow down big army vehicles, such as Humvees. The only way to negotiate them in an elderly BMW was to come at them diagonally, driving very slowly. Failure to do so resulted in a disparaging comment about your driving ability from the client, one hell of a jolt on the descent and the undercarriage of your car having the shit scraped out of it. As the driver of the security vehicle, you could drive any way you wanted. As long as you kept up with the client vehicle and protected it, you were golden.

We arrived at one of the clients' houses around 6.30 a.m. The street looked shabby; everything was covered with dirt and sand. Neighbouring houses had been partially knocked down by shells and there were some building works going on down the road. I stopped my car behind the client vehicle, and Spitfire, my teammate, got out and took up a fire position (a position that provided a good vantage point yet still offered protection from enemy fire).

I stayed in the vehicle, with the engine running and the car in gear. I scanned the road for anything untoward. Meanwhile, Ronin went to get the client and brought him back to his car. Ronin was a friendly Canadian with a great sense of humour. He was an ex–Canadian and British forces soldier who had only recently finished up a contract in Afghanistan, where he'd been working with Spitfire. I liked him as soon as I'd met him.

I followed Ronin's vehicle to the Convention Center and pulled up outside the entrance. Spitfire jumped out of my vehicle and Ronin exited his, escorting the client up to his office while Baloo and I parked our vehicles. After Baloo and I had joined the guys upstairs, Spitfire took me around the Convention Center, showing me the areas I hadn't seen the previous day, leaving the other two to man the security desk.

First, I was shown where all the commissioners worked. The only client in the office was the fellow we'd just picked up. I said hello and introduced myself. He was the head of all the commissioners, so we referred to him as 'Number One'. The other eight commissioners had not yet arrived for work, as they were starting at different times and didn't need us to pick them up. In Iraq, punctuality doesn't hold much cultural value. It didn't take long to realise that whenever someone said they would be at a certain place at a certain time, I had to clarify whether it was 'Iraqi time' or 'our time'.

Next, Spitfire showed me the evacuation route should we ever have to get the clients out of the Convention Center in a hurry. There were numerous twists, turns, stairwells and corridors before we found ourselves outside. I doubted I would remember the route after one walk-through. After retracing our steps, I checked the time: nearly an hour had passed. We went back to the security desk to relieve Baloo and Ronin.

Talking with Spitfire made the time at the desk by go quickly. He was an ex–British Special Forces soldier who had been in the security contractor business for a while. Over the next hour, Spitfire offered a couple of insider tips on how to get by. He said you had to start looking for your next job as soon as you'd signed your current contract. It all came down to networking: that was how you'd find out which contracts were up for grabs, where they'd be happening and which companies were involved. The more people you made friends with, the better your chance of being offered another job when your contract ended. And contracts ended all the time.

Sometimes your contract would just expire, sometimes you were fired for one reason or another, and sometimes you'd just get to the point where you had to move on. If the person running your team didn't like you, it was likely that you'd get sacked at some stage. It didn't matter how good you were at the work: it all ran on personalities. Spitfire said it was all too easy to clash with someone, only to find yourself having to look for a new job. There were so many thundering egos and differing cultures that conflict was inevitable. I thanked Spitfire for the heads-up, not knowing how handy it would prove to be later on.

Still, all this seemed foreign to me. It did my head in thinking about an industry in which conflict was so ingrained. In the army, a good leader would identify those differences, deal with any issues before they became intractable, and then bind all the members together to make a formidable team. A good leader would identify people's flaws and work on turning them around. They would recognise team members' strengths and make the most of them in achieving the mission.

We finished up at about 5 p.m. After dropping Number One back at his house, we drove home, arriving just in time for an orders group. An orders group is a meeting where the leaders pass on information pertaining to the following day's activities. It is also the forum whereby the team is able to raise important issues as well. We quietly joined the rest of team in the lounge room and listened in. Our project manager, Sim, was running through our tasks for the next couple of days; it all sounded fairly routine. He also mentioned that a major task was coming up, but there was something in his tone that struck me as odd, as though he was uncomfortable at the idea. Sim was an ex–Aussie special forces officer, and I trusted him implicitly. Then Sim announced that there'd be a barbecue that night, which we were all to attend. The company was supplying free food and booze for everyone.

It was a Thursday night, and I thought organising a piss-up on a weeknight was strange. Ghost explained that the Iraqi week ran from Sunday to Thursday; Friday and Saturday were the weekend. It felt peculiar to be drinking in a war zone, though. I was still green from my time in the army, where drinking on operations is a big no-no. I reminded myself that I was a civilian now. So I followed suit.

The barbecue was on the rooftop of the company's headquarters in an adjacent street. We all walked over together. On the rooftop a huge spit roast was cooking in the corner. There was an Esky full of beer, and Ghost handed me a can as soon as I arrived. All around me were men drinking like it was their last day on Earth.

There were several other teams present, but they kept to themselves. Although we were all from the same company, there were some 'inter-racial' issues going on. A few members of my team seemed to have something against the Americans. I'd almost go so far as to say they were racist. I don't how else to explain it. Some thought the Americans were too gung-ho and their tactics were too aggressive. A few of the Brits on my team didn't like Americans because their ideology and values differed to their own. They told me that, until I'd worked with a mixed-culture team, I couldn't understand the fundamental differences.

I thought this kind of attitude had been stamped out years before. It definitely wouldn't have been tolerated in the Australian Army. I decided I wasn't going to be part of their war. I'd make friends with whoever I wanted, and judge people on the basis of their personalities, their skills and the value they could add to a team.

I slowly sipped my beer. It was nice to have a drink, but I didn't want to down too many. I was still a newbie and I didn't know my colleagues very well. Ghost brought me over another drink before I'd finished my last, while the other team members filled me in on some of the team gossip.

Just before I'd arrived, two women on my team had been fired. I was told that they were flirty pissheads, and not up to the job. Considering these guys were getting smashed right in front of me, I disregarded the comment about the women being drunkards. I was, however, curious to hear about the women's tactical skills. Ghost said the problem was that the women had had minimal experience with high-powered weapons and were struggling to use them. The truth was that before starting with the company they had been civilian bodyguards working the London circuit.

I was gobsmacked. How the hell did someone without military experience get a job in a combat zone? Putting unskilled operators on the team endangered the client, the team and the women themselves. It was probably for the best that they'd been turfed. As for the tales of their drinking and flirting, I was sceptical. Guys tend to exaggerate details like that, especially if the woman in question isn't flirting with them. There are two sides to every story, and the women's was never told.

By now most of my teammates were well and truly relaxed. Money Shot came over to tell me I would have no problems on the team if I kept going the way I had been over the past week. I had already zeroed my weapon and conducted a marksmanship shoot for the team's project manager. Sim was impressed with my results, as I'd kicked the butts of most of my teammates. The other team leaders said they were happy with my performance and considered me an asset. I was feeling very good at this stage. It felt as though I'd been accepted as a member of the team, and that I could be relied on to do my job.

I was halfway through my second can of beer when it was decided that the team would go to a bar. We drove a short distance to the Bunker Bar, a privately owned establishment located within the Green Zone. As soon as I got out of the car, I could hear the *thump-thump* of a bassline.

The walls inside the bar were lined with decommissioned weapons. I considered them precious antiques and wished I had a collection of them on my walls at home. The bar was jam-packed with other civilian security teams. There was only one other woman there. I felt a little intimidated.

Being the only PSD chick the men would have seen in a while, I was attracting a lot of attention. I kept close to my teammates. Ghost began introducing me to other teams as his wife. I played along; it was the easy option for keeping unwanted guys away.

Eventually we called it a night and went back to the team house. It had been fun. I had got to know my teammates better and it seemed as though we'd be able to gel. I could also tell that Ghost was developing a tiny crush on me, but I wasn't interested in any entanglements just yet. It was more important to be taken seriously as one of the team.

Romance could wait a little longer. Even though it had been more than three years since Bruce had broken up with me, I was still terrified of taking a chance with someone else. Heartbreak is brutal. I had to be sure before I got involved. Ghost seemed nice, but he also came across as a player. Did I really want to get mixed up with a guy like that?

*

One night, a week or so after the barbecue, Sim gave us a heads-up about the major task he'd mentioned. It was our first big operation: one of our clients had a meeting in Kirkuk, a city in northern Iraq, and we had to get him there safely. Details were still sketchy at this stage. It would be up to Sim's second-in-command, Smokey, to flesh out the plan. Smokey had spent many years working as part of a high-profile American organisation. He had been highly decorated for his work and was well respected in those circles. Smokey was under a lot of pressure from the company directors to make this mission happen, but even so his tactical approach was greatly flawed.

The plan involved the CAT, the client, Smokey and me flying into Kirkuk on a military helicopter. The rest of the team were to drive in their soft-skinned vehicles so that the client would have something to drive around in. As the commander of the CPP unit in the Australian Army, these kinds of operations were my bread and butter. My blood ran cold when I heard these orders. Kirkuk was practically the wild west, and the route between it and Baghdad was nicknamed 'the road of death'. Militant groups stalked the road and ambushes, kidnappings and worse were commonplace.

It was suicide to have the team drive all the way to Kirkuk in soft-skinned vehicles. Our contract had major military support allocated to it for exactly these kinds of missions. Where were the armoured vehicles? Why weren't we arguing for the meeting to be moved to a safer place? If there was really no way around it, then surely the CAT should travel by road with them. If our team was attacked on the road, there would be no backup forces, and no reaction force to come to their rescue. They would be literally on their own.

I had to talk to Sim. From a couple of conversations we'd shared, I got the impression he had been unsure about the mission from the start. We had a very frank chat and he understood my concerns straightaway. He had tried to have the operation cancelled due to its risky nature, but the company was not going to have a bar of it. The company had only recently won the contract and did not want to refuse the first major task the commissioners had requested. Sim was told that the Kirkuk trip would go ahead as planned. In consolation, the team was given one armoured vehicle. It was to be used to transport the client once he arrived in Kirkuk.

The rest of the operation's planning was shambolic. People were being switched between vehicles and positions. No one really understood just what was going on. I was cut from the team with a few others at the last moment, but the rest of the guys had to see it through. Security contractors will usually do whatever they are asked to, no matter how perilous or unsafe. No one wants to be thought of as a scaredy cat.

The team arrived back safely from Kirkuk two days later. Sim resigned soon after. He said he wasn't willing to be part of a company that placed its employees in dangerous situations just to curry favour with clients. There were other ways of completing the mission, but the company had not been willing to listen.

As the project manager, Sim was responsible for the safety and welfare of the team. It was his job to ensure the missions were well planned and executed. The heads of the company effectively took that power away from him. As a leader, you must be able to live with the decisions you make and their consequences. Evidently, Sim couldn't live with the choices he'd been forced to make.

The guys came home in one piece and that was what mattered

to me at the time. They each swore they'd never, ever go on a mission like that again. They had been lucky that time, but luck doesn't last forever.

One night, as the team was sitting in the lounge room receiving orders for the next day, a huge *boom* tore through the night air. The windows shook and the sound reverberated around the room. I braced myself for the onslaught of more mortar rounds, and, sure enough, they fell. There had been several mortar attacks over the past week, with shells falling close to the commissioners' workplace – so close, in fact, that standing outside the Convention Center, I could see the wisps of smoke rising from where they'd landed.

I didn't know if it was the still of the night that made this one seem so near, or if it had indeed landed just outside our house. Our new project manager, Cat, ordered us to check on our clients living in the Green Zone. A team of us armed ourselves to the hilt and donned helmets and body armour before getting into two of our vehicles. There's nothing like leaving the relative safety of bricks and mortar and stepping into a soft-skinned vehicle during a mortar attack to get the blood going.

We turned into the street where three of our clients lived, and were met immediately by US military forces. A mortar had landed right in the middle of the street, causing massive destruction. Smokey got out of the car, lit up a cigarette and began taking photos of the area. The rest of us provided perimeter protection. I crouched down next to a fence and awaited further orders, but none ever came. Smokey was busy talking to the clients and taking snapshots.

A female client, Number Three, had been visiting her house to check on how renovations were progressing, as she was hoping to move into it soon. Her timing had been bad. As soon as the mortar hit she fled back to the Red Zone. Our Number Two client, who lived a few doors down, had taken off in his car to God knows where, presumably somewhere safer than his house. Our Number One client wasn't too fazed by what had happened. He didn't want to be moved from his home to a safer building, and insisted on staying.

It was incredible that we were in charge of the commissioners' safety, yet had only limited influence over their movements. Two commissioners had taken off into the unknown, and the third wouldn't budge from his own home, despite the danger. They did their own thing, and only fell under our protection when it suited them. I really struggled with this part of the work, but Baghdad was the clients' home, and they knew it better than us. They trusted us and I supposed we had to trust them too.

Ghost came to check on me and said that the mortar had landed right near Number One's house. A guard had been hit in the neck by some shrapnel from the blast and a child who had been playing outside had also been hurt. I felt a mother's pity for that innocent little boy.

While I waited for Smokey to finish sucking on his cancer stick, I noted a man running towards a small group of people who had gathered in the street. He was dressed in a long white robe splattered with mud. I looked closer to see that it wasn't mud, but blood. I heard a great scream, followed by wailing. Several women, covered from head to toe in black, huddled together and began keening. The sound vibrated throughout the cold night air. Something bad had happened.

The sorrowful howl didn't stop. It grew louder and louder, and steadily more hysterical. A US military interpreter went over to the women, but they were in no condition to talk. The blood-soaked man told him that the little boy who had been playing outside when the mortar hit had died on the way to hospital.

I could only imagine how those women felt. The pain must have been unbearable. I could feel it digging into my heart. If anything like that ever happened to Kane, I wouldn't have hesitated to exact my revenge.

The wailing continued, and eventually Smokey signalled for everyone to head back to the team house. We hadn't been home more than ten minutes when another three mortars hit. Straightaway we were in the vehicles again, driving to the commissioners' street. This time, one of the mortars had landed on Number Two's house.

At least we knew that Number Two, who was still at large, hadn't been blown to smithereens. Number One still refused to leave his home and no amount of convincing by Smokey would make him budge. There was nothing more we could do. Not wanting to stick around a mortar drop zone in our soft-skinned vehicles, we returned to the house. There were no more mortar attacks that night, and all the commissioners lived to tell the tale.

From then onwards, each night before we went to bed we had to physically check on all the commissioners living in the Green

Zone. I am sure this annoyed the commissioners. I know I would have been irritated if I had a security team interrupting my family dinner each night to see if I was still breathing.

One night, Spitfire and I were tasked to perform the check. By this stage, we were no longer knocking on the commissioners' doors and disturbing their family time. We basically just did a drive-by to see that things looked okay. After completing the check, we turned onto the main road and drove towards our team house. It was 9 p.m. and there were not many cars or people about. The US military had imposed a curfew, and if you travelled at night you risked being shot at or arrested. An American civilian had been shot at the previous night. He wasn't killed, but it proved that the military was serious about enforcing the curfew.

We weren't too far from home when large number of cars pulled out from a side street. They sped up until they were right behind us, and started driving in an erratic fashion – fishtailing all over the road with their horns honking. I looked behind us: Iraqis were hanging out of the car windows, yelling, screaming and throwing their arms around in the air. There were about ten vehicles in total, and they took up the whole road. I pulled my AK-47 close to me, but there wasn't much I could do with it while I was driving.

Spitfire grabbed his weapon and released the safety catch, although he kept it low and out of sight of the other drivers. I kept the vehicle steady and continued on our route back to the team house – any sign that we were panicking could have bad consequences. We couldn't identify any weapons in their vehicles so we didn't want to fire any warning shots.

I was feeling tense by now. It was dark, we were alone and being trailed by wild Iraqis. As the cars caught up to us, they began to surround our vehicle. I looked out my window and an

Iraqi man called out to me. He spoke in Arabic and I didn't understand a word but he looked excited and happy. The honking increased and more cars overtook us.

These people were not insurgents; they were wedding guests. It was Eid, the end of Ramadan, and they were celebrating someone's marriage. The wedding party took off, still honking, and disappeared into the night. Spitfire and I both breathed a sigh of relief.

As time went on, I began to settle into a routine. Often I'd be rostered on to do the security picquets at the Convention Center. On my days off, I'd hit the gym, write long emails to Kane and watch old *Star Trek* episodes on DVD. It was strange how quickly living in a war zone became ordinary.

There were some differences between how my life had been and how it was now. Ghost was openly flirting with me, which I wasn't completely averse to. It was nice to have some male attention – it had been years since I'd been in that situation. I didn't turn many heads back home, but, all of a sudden, it was like I was the most desirable person in the country. As one of the very few Western women around, I had the sense I could have had a face like a shoe and yet still found someone interested in me. The attention by Ghost was flattering and overwhelming. I didn't really know how to handle it so I kept things light between us and just focused on my job.

There was plenty to keep me occupied. Number Two was flying out of the country and needed to be taken to the airport: it was time for a BIAP run. I tied my headscarf around my neck, ensuring it was tightly secured. I felt a little limited in terms of head movement but, once I got used to it, I was fine. I hopped in the back seat of the advance vehicle with Spitfire, and we arranged our kit so we could access it easily. As we were wearing our body armour and chest webbing, and carrying an assortment of weapons, it was an extremely squashy fit. After piling the medical kit and spare ammunition onto the seat between us, our movement became even more restricted.

We made ourselves as comfortable as we could, and then Merlin and Swamp jumped in the front. Swamp was an ex–British forces guy in his early twenties. He was extremely smart and planned on studying medicine once he finished his contract in Iraq. He was a terrific team member: incredibly switched on, understood orders, and could be relied on to make good judgment calls. Swamp was the soldier that every commander wanted on their team.

With Swamp behind the wheel, we drove to Number Two's house to pick him up. As the advance vehicle in our team, we were the first of the three cars in the convoy to pass through the last checkpoint before we left the Green Zone. We drove slowly for the first few hundred metres, making sure the other two cars had made it through okay. Once they had cleared the checkpoint, Swamp stepped on the accelerator and we were off.

I was holding my weapon left-handed. It was one of those awkward things you had to do when sitting on the car's right-hand side. As a rightie, this took a little time to get used to, but there was no way around it: if we were attacked from the right, it was essential that I return fire as quickly as possible.

It wasn't so bad firing left-handed, except for the ejected brass rounds. When you fire a weapon, the brass casing from the ammunition gets ejected out the side of the weapon. If you're right-handed and firing a right-handed weapon, the casing shoots away from you.

Fire that same weapon in your left hand, however, and the hot brass casing can hit you right in the face. A face full of hot brass would be the least of my problems, though, if we were attacked.

"RV one," Merlin said, as we hit Route Irish. "RV two," he continued. 'RV' meant 'rendezvous' in military lingo. In the army, it was typical to identify several landmarks as rendezvous points. Then, in the instance you were attacked and your vehicle disabled, you would return to the last RV point and wait for help to arrive. If after a certain period no one came, you would return to the previous RV. This would continue until either help arrived or you were back in a safe area.

I spoke to Merlin a little later, saying I thought that someone had mixed up their military jargon. The RV points that he called over the radio were landmark checkpoints, not RVs. We were not expected to return to these landmarks if our vehicles were disabled and we were running for our lives. In fact, if we got into trouble, our orders were to commandeer a vehicle and drive away from danger. These landmarks were just checkpoints so that everyone knew where we were located along Route Irish.

Merlin agreed that the terminology was wrong, but told me not to worry about it: it was "just the way things were done". He wasn't exactly interested in taking the issue up with the other team leaders, as it was such a small issue. Well, he was right: it was a minor issue, but it still irked me. It wasn't about using the incorrect terminology. It seemed symbolic of a 'near enough is good enough' approach that pervaded the way the team was run.

After passing 'RV five', we made it to Baghdad airport to drop off our client. We couldn't leave the area until we received confirmation that Number Two was on board his plane. Airlines in Iraq were notorious for overbooking passengers. You may have had a ticket for a flight, but until you were in your seat, there was no guarantee you would be leaving on a jet plane. Even if you did manage to snare a seat, there was no guarantee that the plane would take off on time, if at all. It was common for planes not only to leave several hours late, but also several hours early.

The upshot was that we might have to spend a whole day at the airport. We decided to drive over to another team site, which was located in the BIAP–Camp Victory area. That team, which was also part of our company, was tasked with providing security to communications personnel. Once we arrived, I had a quick look around, and peeked inside one of the buildings. There were two rooms to each building, with a shared toilet–bathroom area. Each room had a cushy-looking double bed, a bedside table and gigantic comfy chair. *Only two people to a bathroom! Pure luxury!*

I was introduced to some of the team members, two of them being a husband–wife team. Maria was a tall and slender woman and her husband, Leon, was short and muscular. Maria was a really good operator: she knew her drills backwards, and was a very good shooter – better than her husband, and most of her team for that matter. She was one of only a tiny number of female security contractors in Iraq. Maria was about to head out on a mission so I didn't get much more than a curt "Hello" from her. It was a shame; I would have loved to talk to her about her experiences in Iraq. I was surprised that the company had hired both her and her husband. Normally these kinds of relationships were frowned on. So many issues and complications can occur when working on the same team as your partner, some of which may ultimately interfere with your ability to do your job.

We hung around for another three hours until we got the call that the client had left. On the route back, Spitfire would travel in the client vehicle, which now had a spare seat. This would allow for better security and extra firepower in the middle car.

It was also a welcome relief for me: I would now have more room to spread out my kit. I could turn and move as freely as I liked. I set myself up comfortably and prepared for the journey home. Swamp, Merlin and I were still in the advance vehicle and would head out first. Jeep, Ronin and Spitfire would go next in the client vehicle, and then Ghost, Dr Evil, Tomahawk, Wolf and Blade would follow behind in the CAT wagon.

The plan was simple: make it back alive.

We drove out hard and fast. We swerved and weaved our way around the traffic, reaching speeds of up to 100 kilometres an hour. Swamp was a great driver and knew just where all the potholes were. Potholes – or, more accurately, roadside bomb holes – were scattered all along Route Irish. There was one near an overpass so huge that you could almost lose a vehicle in it.

As our car reached each bridge or overpass, I heard Merlin call over the radio that it was clear: there were no suspicious vehicles, persons or animals nearby. Traffic was banked up in front of us, and Merlin slowed down. Our convoy began to close up, ready to take a detour if necessary. We were approaching the final overpass when Swamp spotted several figures on top. We didn't know whether they were innocent people out for a walk or insurgents ready to drop a bomb on us.

Merlin alerted the others. We were all to proceed with caution. As the advance vehicle, we had to go under the overpass first. Traffic was heavy so we could only travel very slowly. I looked up and to the rear as best I could, hoping not to see anyone dangling a grenade. We cleared the underpass without incident but only got another 50 metres before we were stopped in traffic.

Behind us, the client vehicle was being closely followed by the CAT wagon. As the vehicles began driving through the underpass, Ronin in the client vehicle and Dr Evil in the CAT wagon thought they saw a person holding something. Both drivers sped up and switched lanes – a good drill for avoiding explosive devices being dropped from above.

Unfortunately, neither of them was in a hurry to drive out of the underpass, certain a grenade would be waiting for them on the other side. I was looking out the rear of our vehicle, and saw how it went down. Ronin slammed on the brakes and there wasn't time for Dr Evil to react. The CAT wagon rammed straight into the back of the client vehicle.

"CAT wagon down. CAT wagon down," I heard Ghost squawk over the radio. "Client vehicle is still up," said Jeep after a prolonged pause. Merlin and I leapt out of our car straightaway. I ran to the side of the road and took up a fire position facing outwards. The wagon was cactus: its front was completely crushed. Merlin and Jeep coordinated a very quick cross-load of stores and equipment from the CAT vehicle.

The client vehicle had only sustained minor damage to its rear, and it was still operable. Within minutes we had cross-loaded everything and were back on the road. We managed to squeeze the extra five people and all their equipment into the two remaining vehicles, but things were very tight. The CAT wagon was left abandoned in the middle of the road, and we took off in a hurry. Route Irish was not a place to dilly-dally.

Back at the team house we quickly offloaded our stores and equipment. Ronin and Jeep were taken to the military hospital. Dr Evil had also hurt himself, but swore he didn't need a doctor.

Ronin had injured his shoulder, and Dr Evil had banged up his knee and knocked his head on the steering wheel.

It was Jeep who I was worried about. He'd blacked out for a few seconds, which was why there had been such a long pause over the radio before he gave us a situation report. His head had hit the dashboard: his cheek was cut and there was bruising all around his eye. Jeep was fast becoming a close friend of mine. He was the second-in-command of all the team leaders and would take over missions when Stu had other things to attend to. He was a big, loud American who had me in stitches a lot. He was rude, tactless and completely obnoxious to the local staff, yet I got on famously with him. He felt sort of like a big brother to me. Later, when he arrived back from the hospital, he was cursing and ranting about having to wear an eye patch. I was happy to see that his humour (and temper) had returned to normal.

While the guys were at the hospital, Stu – our overall team leader – and Smokey busily devised a plan to recover the abandoned CAT wagon. Stu was an ex–British clearance diver and also a combat engineer. He was well educated, had managerial qualifications, and wasn't afraid to speak his mind. Even so, the plan took them all of about five minutes to devise. Six of us were to go back out to the crash site in two vehicles. Once we got there, we'd hook the disabled wagon onto one of the vehicles, and then tow it back to the Green Zone. The second vehicle would provide security.

Dr Evil drove the first vehicle, with Stu and me as the passengers. The brothers, Wolf and Blade, and Smokey travelled in the rear vehicle. We slowly went through the US checkpoint, informing the guards that we were going to recover our disabled vehicle on Route Irish and bring it back to the Green Zone. They thought we were bonkers.

I could see the traffic chaos that the CAT wagon had created from quite a distance away. Cars were banked up as vehicles tried to merge into one lane. Panicked drivers were doing some pretty crazy stuff in order to get off the road. It was bedlam.

We pulled up in front of the wagon. I jumped out to provide observation in front, just as I had been ordered to. Dr Evil had to concentrate on positioning his car so the wagon could be attached for towing. Stu and Smokey were busy searching for bombs that might have been planted on the wagon while we were gone. The two brothers, Wolf and Blade, halted traffic to the rear and provided firepower in that direction. To say the situation was hairy is an understatement.

I spotted a man walking nearby with an AK-47. He wasn't pointing it at us or behaving in a threatening manner, but he was packing and that was threat enough. I alerted the team that I had identified a possible hostile person and to be ready if anything happened. In the meantime, Stu completed the improvised explosive device (IED) check and hooked up the wagon to our vehicle. Once that was done, Stu and Smokey got into the wagon to steer it, stopping it from veering off the side of the road. I heaved a sigh of relief when I heard Stu call for us to withdraw.

Still keeping my eyes on the man with the AK-47, I walked backwards towards my vehicle. Dr Evil had already started the engine and was inching away from the site. He bloody well made me jump into the car while it was moving so I wouldn't be left behind. It must have been quite a sight: this Western chick, armed and kitted up to the max, sprinting after and leaping on board a car rolling away at 5 kilometres an hour. I'm not the most graceful at the best of times, but throw body armour and webbing on me, and there are baby giraffes that move more elegantly.

Dr Evil towed Stu and Smokey in the broken CAT wagon. Wolf and Blade trailed behind us in the rear vehicle. The vehicle recovery had not been ideal. The plan was put together hastily in order to get the vehicle back quickly. There were no contingency plans for if we were attacked on the road or if the CAT wagon detonated while we were recovering it. It was very much a 'fly by the seat of your pants' mission. Fortunately, we arrived back at the team house safely. Dr Evil and I dropped the wagon off at the company's headquarters, where we'd had the barbecue all those weeks ago. Back then, I'd felt so confident about my team. Now I was starting to have my doubts.

I was being rostered on at the Convention Center nearly every day. Between the occasional client moves, we watched movies and mucked around on the internet. The days were a strange mix of being on intense alert, looking out for threats, and being profoundly bored. One evening, after a long day at the office, Merlin informed me that I was needed for a major mission. Our female client, Number Three, was giving a lecture at the University of Baghdad, and I would be her personal bodyguard. I was ecstatic: at last, I'd be used in a real close protection role and not just on some cowboy security task. This was what I had trained for.

The University of Baghdad was located a few kilometres into the Red Zone. I would join a reconnaissance party first thing the next morning. Number Three would be giving her speech in what was known unnervingly as 'the Red Room'. We needed to make sure we were familiar with the site in order to make all the security arrangements for the mission.

As I was learning, things in my team never seemed to go smoothly. That night, I was told I would be used as the bodyguard who handled 'female' issues and that Smokey would be used as the 'real' bodyguard. If anything were to happen, it would be up to Smokey to step in and rescue the client.

What kind of bullshit is this? What do 'female' issues even mean? I asked myself. Either I was used as the bodyguard or I was not. If I was only there to deal with 'lady problems', they should have just kept me as a normal team member. I was a fully trained bodyguard and my training was far superior to anyone else's on the team. I was done biting my tongue.

I walked up to Merlin and told him that 'job sharing' the bodyguard duty was not on. Merlin argued that I would do everything a normal bodyguard would, except that Smokey would take over if anything untoward happened to the client. I told him that not only was it insulting to me, it was also unprofessional and potentially dangerous. What if I made the call that the client should be moved and Smokey disagreed? Whose assessment would take precedence? That sort of ambiguity in a dicey situation could prove fatal. No matter how I phrased it, Merlin just couldn't see what my problem was – why I would take issue with not being trusted to do my job, despite the indisputable fact I was the best qualified person on the team to do it. I had to fall into line in the end, as unhappy about the decision as I was.

The next morning, seven of us trekked out to the University of Baghdad. Merlin and I were in the advance vehicle with a couple of other guys, and the CAT followed close behind. Being but a humble shooter in the rear of the vehicle, I was not given a map. Apparently, they were in short supply; it seemed an odd thing to skimp on. I had my personal GPS (a device used for navigating), so if I somehow got lost on the ground, at least I'd be able to find my way back to the Green Zone. Although, I'd been warned that the signal in this area was often patchy or completely unavailable.

Having trust in your team members is a big deal when they are navigating. In this case, Merlin was the man with the map. In the beginning, Merlin appeared to know where he was going, but it didn't take long to realise that he was lost. Actually, 'lost' is too harsh a word. He wasn't lost; he just couldn't find the place we were looking for. He was trying to locate the security team that was providing protection to the International Republican Institute (IRI) members. Their site was in the Red Zone, a short distance away from the university.

The IRI security team was also attending Number Three's lecture, and Merlin wanted to liaise with them on a few issues. Merlin frantically made phone calls to his contact, trying to work out where we were in relation to him. The contact guided us to their team site. There, Merlin spoke to the IRI guys for several minutes before we left for the university. This time there were no problems finding the place. We drove through the front gates and, following a few directions from local security staff, we found at the Red Room.

Merlin and Mr Happy, an Irish guy on the team, got out of the car to do a quick recon of the place. The rest of us were told to stay outside with the vehicles and be ready in case anything happened. While we waited, an Iraqi man came up to us. I tensed for a moment but he just wanted to talk. Although I didn't understand much of what he was saying, it was clear he was making friendly conversation.

We told him we had to go when we spied Merlin and Mr Happy exiting the building. Our new mate gestured excitedly and seemed to ask us to wait a few minutes. The man raced off towards a nearby building, while Mr Happy took a few photos of the outside area. Not everyone goes on the reconnaissance trip so photos and film footage need to be brought back in order to brief the rest of the team. The more comprehensive the photos and the brief, the better prepared the whole team will be for the security task.

Back in our vehicles, we slowly began to drive away. The Iraqi man we had been speaking to rushed out of the building and tried to flag us down. He was holding two piles of what looked like roughly cut paper. Merlin rolled down his window a few inches and instantly we were overcome with the aroma of freshly baked bread. Merlin rolled his window down lower, and the man handed him two loaves.

We thanked him sincerely, our mouths watering. We stuffed the crusty warm bread into our mouths as we drove out of the university. It was difficult to look fierce and threatening with chipmunk cheeks full of delicious bread. The taste was too divine for me to care very much.

We arrived back at the team house and Merlin and Ghost went off to talk to Jeep, Smokey, Stu and Cat about the mission. As I took my kit off, I thought about just how top-heavy this team was. The command staff nearly outnumbered us proles. At orders, we were told our company headquarters was so excited about the task that the country manager had decided he wanted to be a part of team too. He was to be used as a sniper. I thought his sniper days were well and truly behind him, and that he'd be better off in his air-conditioned office, working on getting us some armoured vehicles.

It was getting late. Orders had finished and I was gearing up for my first major mission. The next day I would finally put my hard-earnt skills to the test: I was going to protect my female client on a real mission. I went to bed early, as I wanted to get a good night's rest. As I was settling into bed, my phone beeped a couple of times: it was Ghost sending a few saucy text messages. I still didn't know if I liked it or not. It was flattering, but dangerous. He was a team leader, and he struck me as the sort of man who didn't like it when things didn't go his way. I texted Ghost back but kept my response breezy.

I was playing with fire.

The next morning, while still lying in bed, I carefully went through a million different scenarios in my head.

Some deep insecurities surfaced, but I had to push them aside. This was no time for self-doubt. I told myself that I was good enough for the job – that, in fact, I was the most qualified, most experienced and best suited person for this particular job. It was my opportunity to show the guys on my team that I was their equal. I was not some pathetic little girl just there as a token. I was going to prove beyond doubt that I was a valuable member of the team; I'd show them my worth.

I stared blankly into my wardrobe. My teammates were going to be dressed in highly visible combat gear: webbing, rifles and their usual 'war fighting' rig. Whereas it had been decided that I would go low profile. Openly armed security personnel would not be allowed inside the auditorium while Number Three was delivering her lecture, as such an aggressive display would send the wrong message. That meant that my teammates – and all their kit – would have to remain outside the building.

I pulled out a pair of black suit pants and a conservative blouse. I concealed my pistol in my waistband and wore thick body armour over my torso. If the shit hit the fan, at least I would be able to shield Number Three with my body. My pistol provided only limited weapon capability, but it would hold me over until my teammates stormed the building and evacuated us.

I was set.

At one o'clock we drove over to the commissioners' workplace. Stu and I walked into the building, with an extra suit of body armour for Number Three. As we strode through the corridors, office workers began to chatter to each other and look at us. They knew something was going on. We knocked on Number Three's door and told her it was time to leave.

In an effort to be warm and welcoming, Stu attempted to shake hands with her. Immediately, Number Three shrieked and hid behind me. In Islam, touching a member of the opposite sex to whom you are not related is prohibited. I was surprised that this had not been part of the briefing. Stu apologised profusely and handed me the body armour before quickly leaving the room.

I explained to Number Three that I had some body armour, which would protect her while she was out in the Red Zone. I asked if she'd put it on. I might as well have asked her to dance for me. It didn't matter how much I told her about the risk, she was adamant that she was not going to wear it. I radioed through to Stu to tell him what was going on. He came in and also tried to persuade Number Three to wear the body armour, but again she refused.

As security personnel, we have a duty of care to encourage the client in the strongest possible terms to wear the protection for their own safety. If a client refuses, there isn't much to be done about it: they are the ones paying the bills. I warned Number Three that her level of protection would be lower than if she wore the armour. I don't know if it interfered too much with the placement of her head scarf, or if she just felt too embarrassed to wear it public when other Iraqis had no protection? Either way, she would not be swayed.

Stu and I escorted Number Three down to the waiting vehicle. Stu said I'd have to share the back seat with her, thanks to there being 'two bodyguards'. This wasn't normal, and went against everything I knew to be the best way to keep our client safe. Smokey would sit in the front, ready to react if 'something happened'.

I was still unclear on what my role was supposed to be in that situation. If the shit hit the fan, my first reaction would be to cover Number Three. There was no way I would just hide and wait for Smokey to take over. I talked it over with Stu and he understood. As far as he was concerned, Smokey was just along for the ride.

At the university, we got out of the vehicle and I started to escort Number Three to the Red Room. Usually a bodyguard will walk slightly behind the client, remaining as unobtrusive as possible. Number Three didn't want me walking behind her; she wanted me right next to her. That was fine with me: it meant I could provide far better protection for her. At times she would even hold my arm to keep me close. It was plain to see that having a woman on the team was invaluable. We had built up a rapport and she trusted me. Number Three felt happy and safe with me because we were both women.

It can be intimidating and off-putting to be surrounded by so many big, fierce-looking men. If I – a strong-willed woman who has worked with men for many years – could feel that way at times, I could only imagine how someone like Number Three would feel. At any rate, having me around made the client feel a lot more comfortable, and seeing her vulnerable like that just made me feel more protective of her. She was my client, she needed me, and I would protect her. I wouldn't let her down.

We entered the Red Room, and straightaway people swarmed around Number Three. Locals in their dozens had turned up to listen to her presentation, and wanted to have a few words with her. As the audience took their seats, I stood off to the side of the room, still within five metres of Number Three. Before the speech kicked off, I had been offered a seat several times. I initially refused, wanting to be ready to spring into action should something happen. I soon realised, however, that it was far better just to accept their generosity.

As Number Three delivered her presentation, I studied each member of the crowd. I looked for concealed weapons, agitated faces and restlessness. Some of them were busy studying me back, but most were focused on Number Three. She received thunderous applause at the end of her speech. Everyone wanted to thank her, but time was slipping away. She told me she wanted to leave so I carefully blocked her fans with my body and ushered her out of the building. As it turned out, I didn't have to worry about that issue with Smokey. During the operation, he didn't go anywhere near the client. He just stood outside, lighting up fag after fag.

The cars were outside waiting for us. We got into the vehicles and slowly rolled out of the university. We dropped Number Three back off at work. I walked her up to her office and she looked into my eyes and thanked me for being with her. I said goodbye and left, smiling to myself.

The day had gone well. I felt I had cemented my position on the team. My teammates even commented that they hadn't realised I was so switched on. I chose to take that as a compliment, but really I was just happy that my skills were being put to good use.

It was another run-of-the-mill day at the commissioners' workplace, except that it was Thanksgiving. I walked across to the Al Rasheed with a couple of the American guys for lunch. After waiting in an extremely long queue, behind hundreds of soldiers, I was stunned when I entered the food hall. Streamers in red, white and blue were strung along the walls. Tables overflowing with food were everywhere: they were covered with turkey, baked potatoes, cranberry sauce and pecan pies. There were ice sculptures, butter sculptures, gingerbread houses and cakes. Thanksgiving was something I had only ever seen on sitcoms. I treasured sharing this occasion with my American teammates. Together we gave thanks for the wonderful food we were served, the friends we had made and our safety in Iraq so far.

I sat down with the two brothers, Wolf and Blade, as well as another guy named 51-50, who was a dead spit for Vin Diesel, with a tough exterior but a heart of gold. Ghost was always giving him shit about looking too gung-ho on the road: 51-50 refused to dress in local get-up, preferring to wear his protective kit and carry numerous weapons as overtly as possible. I didn't agree with Ghost; 51-50's appearance was in line with his job. He worked as part of the heavy weapons section of the CAT. They had to be gunned up and ready to impose massive amounts of firepower in order to get the rest of us out of the shit if insurgents struck. Besides, he was concealed in the back of the wagon. Who was going see him? I thought the reason Ghost didn't like him was that 51-50 was an ex–navy SEAL, and very experienced in the world of security contracts. Perhaps there was some jealousy at play.

A few months back, 51-50 had been a member of a team providing security to a convoy travelling across the Iraqi desert. His team (or, more specifically, his vehicle) was hit with an IED. As he had been the only team member wearing full protective equipment, including hearing protection, 51-50 found himself the only one capable of reacting. When the noise of the explosion reverberated throughout the vehicle, shock set in and the 'fog of war' descended, leaving the other teammates stunned.

But 51-50 was able to fire back at the insurgents (most IED attacks are followed by small-arms fire). He was then able to drag his mates to safety before the other vehicles in his team came to his aid. Ghost could say whatever he wanted about 51-50, but it fell on deaf ears as far as I was concerned. Despite 51-50's tough appearance, his personality was completely different. He was really quite in touch with his spiritual side, and was just a nice guy. Thanksgiving was one of the best days I had with my teammates.

Ghost, Merlin and Stu were due to fly out soon. They were all taking leave over the Christmas period, and there had been a mad scramble to appoint replacements when they realised at the last minute that their dates overlapped. It seemed problematic to have three team leaders on leave at the same time, but what did I know.

Jeep would take over from Stu as the overall team leader. Silver, a short, medium-build man in his forties, would become the advance team leader and Wolf the CAT commander. There was also the problem of what to do with their kit. Normally, it would be packed up, and when the person returned, they'd unpack their stuff wherever a spare bed was available.

The old team leaders weren't happy with that idea. They wanted to come back to their original beds. They didn't want to risk having to share a room with the other teammates, especially the Americans, after they came back. Already they driven Mr Happy out of their room as the guys kept making derogatory comments towards him. Ghost and Merlin put their heads together and came up with a solution: I was turfed out of my room, and moved into theirs. They argued that because I was close friends with them and Jeep, who they also shared with, they were suitable roommates. That way, they would be able to keep their beds free, as it was not appropriate that I share a room with anyone else. To give me some privacy, Merlin rearranged a couple of cupboards and strung up a curtain to screen off my small corner. I did still count these boys as my good friends, but there was something cavalier and unthinking about the way they were acting. The only things they considered when making decisions were matters that directly affected them.

Stu, Ghost and Merlin left the country the morning after they'd come up with the room-swap idea, and Jeep and I were left bunking together. Ghost hugged me goodbye, and whispered that he'd email me while he was gone, something I was not bothered about either way. I sort of liked him, but sort of didn't. I did not want to confuse the feeling of being wanted with love.

*

Jeep was now in charge. As he was my friend and now roommate, I thought the new command structure would give me the chance to have some subtle input on tactical matters. Jeep could choose to use my advice or ignore it, of course, but at least it wouldn't feel quite as if I was just yelling into the void.

That was not how things worked out. It was Silver who ended up really running the team. He was good friends with Jeep, but could recognise that his mate struggled with command issues. Every night, Silver would take Jeep through the rotation of personnel working at the Convention Center. The simple act of staff rostering was too much for our team leader, and recording it on a spreadsheet was downright impossible. I assisted Jeep with all things to do with the computer, while Silver wrote orders on a whiteboard for Jeep to recite.

It was not so bad to start off with, but things steadily grew worse. All the paperwork and other admin slipped through the cracks. The Americans were no longer accepting passports for entry into their gym facilities, and the company could not organise alternate passes for us. No gym facilities meant no fitness training. I was desperate to keep up my fitness level, so I'd do whatever necessary to ensure it was maintained. That said, I didn't have a death wish. I was not going to put myself in an unsafe position by running around the Green Zone. Instead, I ran up and down our 200-metre-long street. It was less than ideal: the street was close to a dirt track and often very muddy; the generators ran nonstop outside the houses, filling the air with smoke fumes; and the local security guards would stare at me.

Frustrated at being gawked at like a freak, I changed to running up and down the stairs at the house. There were four flights of stairs and the rooftop, where I could do circuit training afterwards. Tomahawk, a Native American guy on my team, would practise his knife-fighting drills on the roof, as I skipped, did push-ups and squats, and shuttle ran to the music on my iPod.

Tomahawk was a quiet man, and he looked out for me. He was separated with two lovely children back in America. He wanted to earn as much as possible so that he could put them through college and give them a good life. One day, he showed me a letter he had written for his kids and some sacred items he wanted passed on to his children should anything happen to him in Iraq. He had a ritual involving these keepsakes that he would follow each time he left on a mission.

I was very touched that he had shared something so special and personal. We often spoke about our kids and how much they meant to us. I told Tomahawk that I had written two letters that would go to my son in the event I was killed in Iraq: a child's version; and another that he could read after he turned eighteen. There are some things that can't be explained to a child. I told Tomahawk that writing those letters was the hardest thing I had ever done.

Tomahawk looked at me with knowing eyes. He seemed to understand a lot more than he let on. He told me that my son loved me and that I would be with him again. He then gave me a set of rosary beads his boy had made at school. He wanted me to have them for good luck and as a reminder of our friendship. It was a moment I would remember for the rest of my life.

A week or so before Christmas, I got wind of a big operation: our female client, Number Three, was giving another talk about the upcoming Iraqi elections, this time at the Babylon Hotel. There would be high-ranking Iraqi officials from all over the country attending. The reconnaissance party was to be small: four people, including me, and one vehicle.

The Babylon Hotel was out in the Red Zone. It was only a short distance from the entrance to the Green Zone, but still a long way from help if we needed it. We dressed as discreetly as we could, and attempted to hide our weapons beneath our coats. Now, to hide a pistol is no big deal, but to keep an AK-47 out of sight is a little trickier.

Silver, Baloo, Mr Happy and I all piled into an armoured car. We kept in touch with the team house via mobile phone, an unreliable tool, but it was all we had available to us. No one paid us much attention as we weaved through the heavy traffic. Ours was just another car on the road. After the last checkpoint it wasn't long till I spotted the Babylon Hotel: it was a massive box-shaped building that loomed over the city like a pyramid.

We parked the car, concealed our weapons as well as we could, and made our way into the hotel. Silver took the hotel manager aside to discuss details. I took a look around, as did Baloo and Mr Happy. The hotel was huge, lined with big glass doors and marble floors. None of the amenities seemed as though they'd been replaced in a long while, but everything was kept immaculately clean.

The manager led us to a big auditorium, which was where the meeting would take place. I started filming with the video camera, taking footage of our possible escape routes, safe rooms, and entry and exit points. Satisfied we'd gathered enough information about the area and knew exactly how the operation was going to run, we drove home. Silver took off to prepare the orders for the next day.

The following morning went like clockwork. We'd arrived at the hotel and Number Three was ushered into the auditorium and shown around. She was jumpy and much more nervous than during her last presentation. Number Three made it quite clear to me that no one was to take her photo during her speech. She was absolutely terrified of the ramifications for her family should the local paper print a photo of her, identifying her as a pro-democracy supporter. I informed Jeep of her fears and he assured us both that no photos would be taken. Number Three looked relieved and continued to prepare for her talk.

About an hour into her speech, I noticed one of the audience members begin to fiddle around with a camera bag. As soon as I realised that he was getting ready to photograph Number Three, I motioned to Jeep that he needed to intervene.

Jeep looked at me with a dumb expression on his face and did nothing. I motioned again. I couldn't speak to him. There had not been enough radios to go around, and I had drawn the short straw once again. Jeep was only about 10 metres away from me, but still did not move. I realised he was not going to do anything about the cameraman. I didn't know if Jeep was too shy to walk out in front of the seated audience members and make a fuss, or if he just didn't take the security risk to Number Three seriously. As Number Three's bodyguard, I had to remain close to her at all times. In the end, though, I had to make a decision.

Did I stay by the side of my client and let the photographer do his worst, knowing that this was what she was deathly afraid of happening? Or did I commit a bodyguard no-no and leave her side to confiscate the camera myself? I weighed up the risks and decided that she would be safe for the half a minute it would take to deal with the photographer – but I wasn't happy about it. I would have to trust my team to save Number Three should anything happen during the precious seconds I left her side.

Number Three continued to address the audience as I quietly walked about 10 metres down the centre aisle towards the photographer. As it turned out, Number Three's assistant instantly realised the threat to his boss when he saw me approach the cameraman. He came over quickly to sort out the problem.

Leaving the photographer in the assistant's capable hands, I returned to Number Three's side. I was gone only thirty seconds, but it seemed a lot longer. I was seething at the company for not having enough radios. I was seething at Jeep for not having stopped the photographer himself. I was seething at the other team members for not reacting. There were four other security team members in the room and none of them did anything about the photographer. Jeep could have dealt with the photographer himself, or sent any one of the team members to do it for me. I shouldn't have had to leave my client's side.

I was pretty pissed off at the debriefing when we got back to the team house. Jeep told me I was wrong to leave the client. He was right, but I made it pretty fucking clear that my hand had been forced. He should have done something about it when I indicated the photographer to him in the first place. He knew the client's wishes. He was the leader. Jeep proceeded to blame other members of the team for not intervening, despite their pleas that they hadn't even seen the cameraman. Jeep had a radio and could have easily radioed a member of the team to deal with the situation.

I was getting really frustrated. I was used to the Australian Army. There, we worked as a team; we communicated and we helped each other out. If someone had to deal with a threat, the rest were there to back the member up. This was not how they rolled in this team. No one was being trained properly, people were stepping into jobs they weren't qualified to perform, and there was no group solidarity.

Now my professionalism was being compromised. I was good at my job, but I was having to make decisions I wasn't proud of. Jeep and I made up after the debrief, but I knew things were beginning to change between us.

Jeep was a talker. This quality made him a great drinking buddy but a downright irritating leader. His problem was that he'd prattle on for hours about minor issues during orders group. He would bang on for ages about a scuffed car tyre, or our cleaning staff, or the state of the toilets. Understandably, most of the guys tuned out after the first five minutes of waffling. Silver became more forthright in terms of organising ID cards, missions and people, and eventually was promoted to the role of assistant project manager. It was well earnt. He was doing a good job and making things easier for the rest of the team.

To put an exact date of when things really went downhill is hard. Soon enough, though, we had a situation where the project manager, Cat, couldn't organise regular car maintenance or getting enough food in the house. Well-liked team members were getting all the good missions, while less popular ones were being continually rostered on for picquets at the commissioners' workplace. But that was nothing compared to what I saw going on behind closed doors.

Sharing a room with Jeep, I became privy to a lot of information. I began to understand how political it was running a team. There was pressure to cut costs and increase profits, and someone's ability to gain weapons, ammunition or ID cards could dictate whether they stayed on a team or were shown the door. If you were part of the 'in crowd', you were guaranteed employment regardless of your actual ability. If the right people did not like someone, it was only a matter of time until they were given the boot.

Seeing how the security business ran made me more and more critical of what was going on. I was losing confidence in the guys running this project, and gaining more confidence in my own abilities. Jeep was a great friend, but I now had real doubts about his ability to lead the team. Silver was good at what he did, but he was not without his flaws.

Silver, Jeep and I were sitting in our room one night, having a yarn. Jeep was a great storyteller and a funny bastard, especially after a few drinks: his accent combined with his outrageous personality always made for an entertaining tale. Silver and Jeep began telling stories of the 'good old days' in Iraq, when suddenly Jeep's phone began to ring.

After a short conversation, Jeep announced that Andy was coming over for a few drinks. I hadn't met Andy before. Silver explained that he was a medic working for another security company. Silver didn't have a bad word to say about him. He heaped praise on Andy's ability to assist with medical procedures. He was at pains to say that while Andy was not much for book smarts, he had excellent practical skills and a great memory when it came to performing medical procedures. Silver mentioned that he had plans for using Andy in future work.

Andy arrived about fifteen minutes later. He was a tall bloke, with dark hair and a strong British accent. His eyes were red raw, which I assumed was the result of working many hours in a surgery. He immediately grabbed a drink and sculled it down. *I guess he really needed that!* He grabbed another straightaway, but went a little slower on that one. We sat around drinking as I listened to their stories. It wasn't long before the conversation took a dark turn. One minute Andy was telling us another Jeep story, and the next he was asking for drugs. I was astounded, to say the least, and what happened next changed everything. Silver opened up his wallet and pulled out a neatly folded piece of paper.

I looked on with curiosity as he slowly unfolded the paper. Inside was white powder. Silver tapped it out onto a table and Jeep pulled out a credit card. He then used the card to chop the powder into fat little lines. Everything seemed unreal. Jeep then rolled up an American dollar bill and proceeded to snort the powder up his nose. Andy followed suit, but Silver gave it a miss.

I sat with a blank look on my face, afraid to say something and afraid to say nothing. My friends, my leaders, my teammates were into coke. How often did they take it? Were they drug-affected when we went out on missions? How could they be responsible for the safety and welfare of our team while taking drugs? There had been whispers about steroids making the rounds of the team, but this was shocking. Merlin had alluded to smoking dope at a particular point in time back in Australia. I began to wonder if he was doing it here in Iraq as well. I'd counted these men as good friends and it turned out I didn't know them at all.

It wasn't long before I feigned tiredness and went to bed. Silver, Jeep and Andy continued to drink and talk, as I lay in bed in the corner of the room, my eyes wide open. *What do I do?* Did I rat on my friends? Being the leaders, would they just deny everything? I had seen other contractors speak out and then get sacked. Was I prepared to do the same? I felt so alone. I had given up a promising career in the army for this shit. I was going on leave in a few weeks; I'd just have to hold on till then. I'd keep my mouth shut for now, and take advantage of a fresh perspective after a break away from these dickheads.

Above: A family photo of Lil, Ced, baby Shannon and me, 1979. Mum was always putting Lil and me in matching dresses when were little.

Below: Ced and me climbing a tree when we were kids, 1976.

Left: Completing the Bayonet Assault Course during recruit training, 1993. *(Photo by Freeman's Photographic Services)*

Below: Me after completing a drill (marching) test during recruit training, 1993. *(Photo by Freeman's Photographic Services)*

Opposite: Me during Close Personal Protection Training, 2003. *(Photo by Shannon Joyce)*

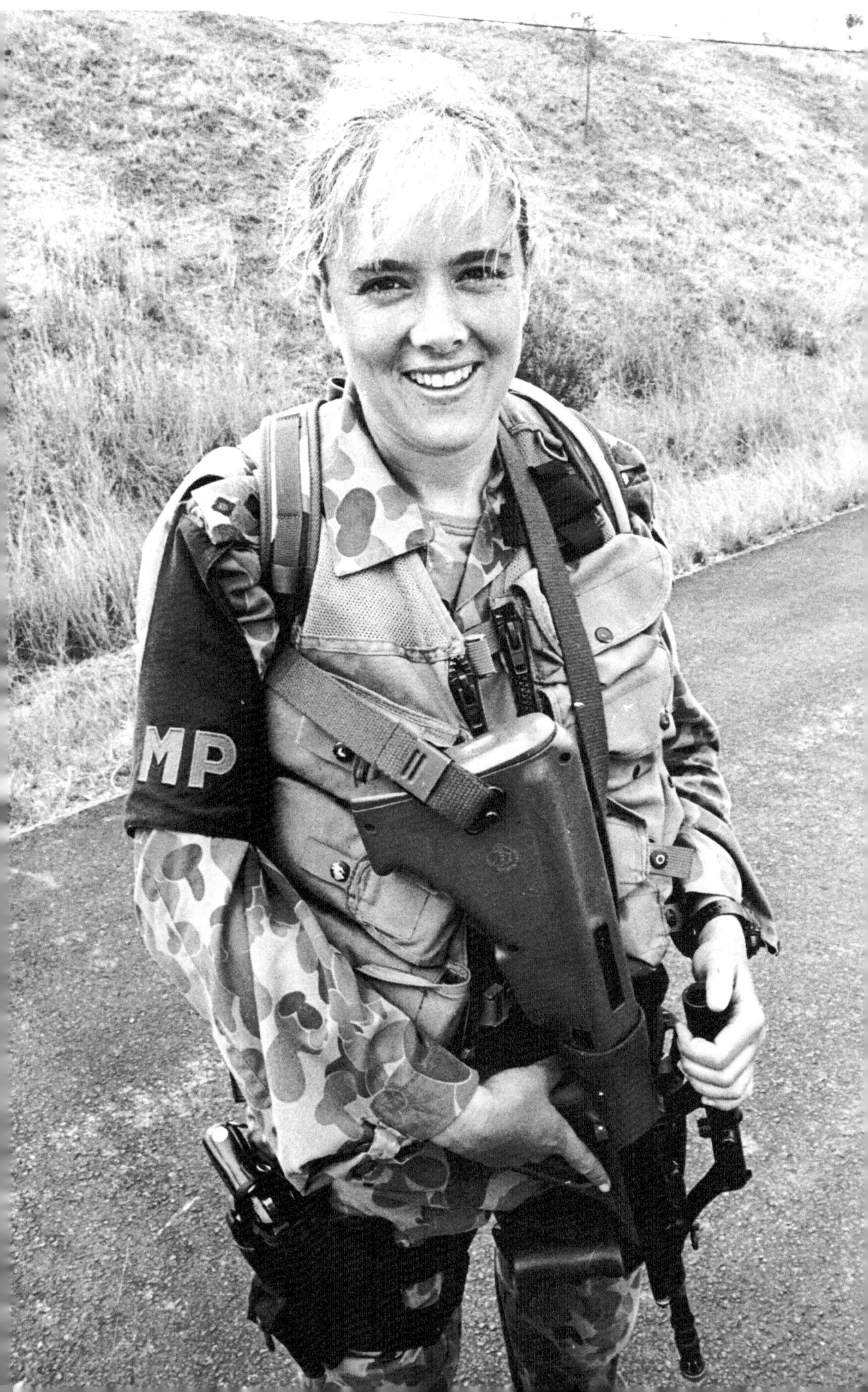
MP

Top: Kane and me on my graduation day from the Royal Military College, 2001.

Middle: Kane's first day at school, 2005.

Below: Mother's Day in Iraq, 2006.

Opposite, top: Having delivered our client safely onto the Blackhawk helicopter in the background, we were off to attend another pre-election meeting in the Red Zone, 2005.

Opposite, below: The clothing I wore when travelling along BIAP Road, Iraq, so I would blend in with the locals, 2004.

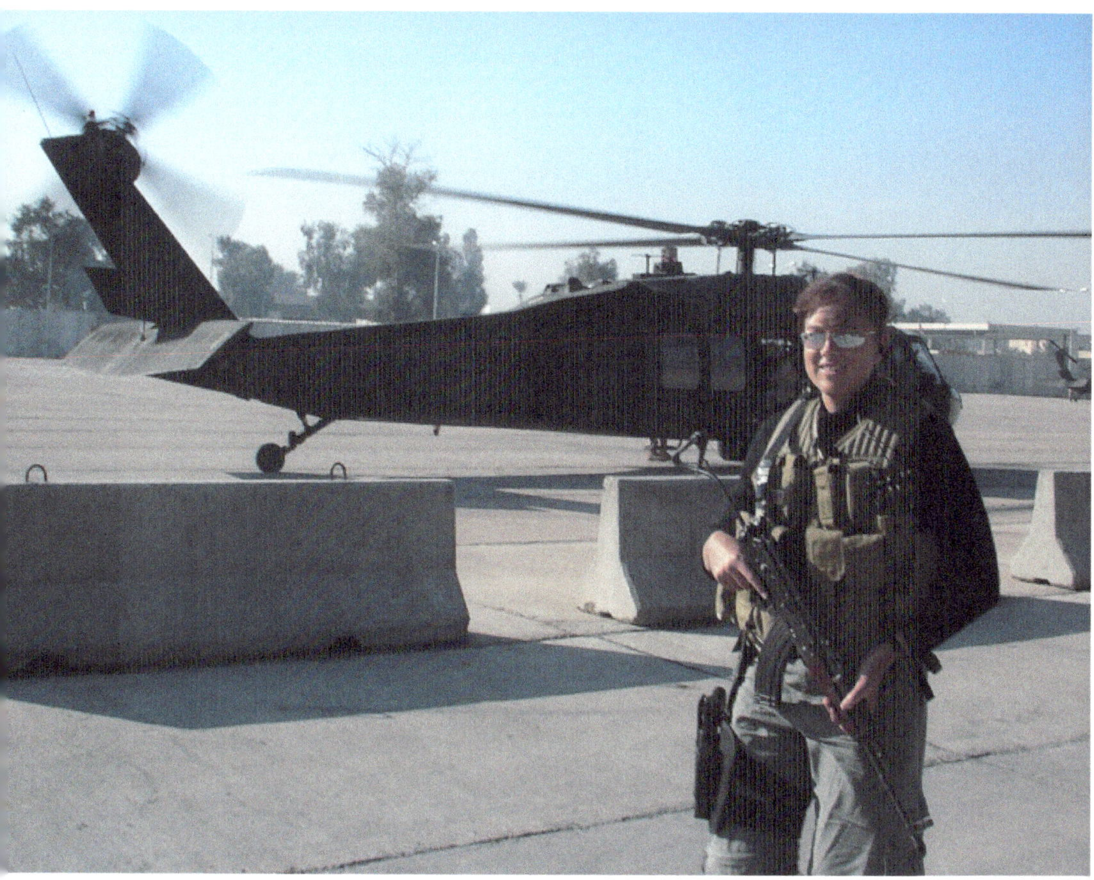

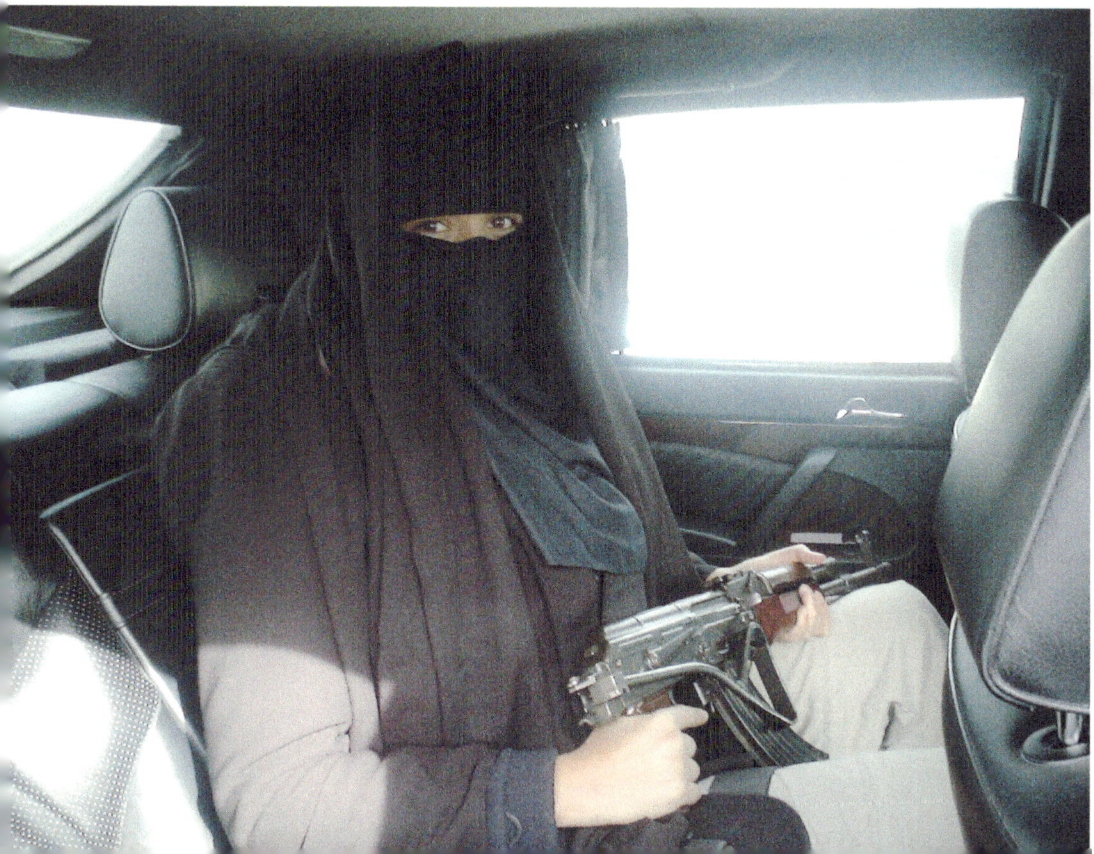

Above: About to leave for a Red Zone mission to the Babylon Hotel with my female client, 2005.

Left: With Mr Happy and Cobra in 2005, waiting for our clients to arrive.

Right: Standing in front of a Blackwater Mamba vehicle (aptly named 'Chick Magnet') in 2005, holding a clip-on koala which I later gave the driver.

Below: On the Ronin close protection course, 2005, and about to head out on an assessed mission with a teammate. I had been appointed Counter Assault Team Leader for the test.

Above: Paul and me in Perth in 2006 – our first time together outside a war zone. We ended up buying a house not far from where this photo was taken.

Left: Paul's kids, Liam and Georgia, with Kane in 2007.

I awoke the next morning, tired and stressed. Everything was bugging me. It was another day at the Convention Center. I was the allocated the position of team leader for the day. Normally, I would have relished the responsibility, but today I looked on the opportunity with disdain. We had four team leaders, all of who were getting paid far more than me, who should have been doing the job. Instead, they were back at the team house mucking around on their computers all day, perving on women's MySpace profiles.

I was tired of putting up with this shit. They were team leaders; they should have been running the picquets and the associated client moves. The pace had been stepped up, and now five or six people were needed to work at the Convention Center. Clients were continually going to important meetings, which meant there was a lot of coordinating of vehicles and people to be done by the person in charge. That person was rarely one of the team leaders. In fact, I was certain Jeep wouldn't have been able to even put a client's name to their face.

My gripes, though, were nothing compared to the bombshell I received later that morning.

Number Three called the security desk at the Convention Center. She was in hysterics. She had just received a call from her old neighbour. The neighbour told her that insurgents had stormed his apartment, beaten up his family and held them at gunpoint. They had demanded to know where Number Three was living: she was their intended target.

Number Three had only just moved her family into their refurbished Green Zone residence two days before. If they had not moved, her whole family would have been killed. It was a shocking realisation. The neighbour had rung Number Three to let her know that their lives had been spared, but they were frightened and hurt. I called Jeep to let him know what had happened, hoping he would step up security for Number Three.

When we arrived home from the Convention Center later that evening, the news didn't get any better. An insurgent had been captured and handed over to the US military in the vicinity of our team house. It was my American teammate, Outpatient, who found and then detained the insurgent. Outpatient was one hell of a tall and gangly man. He was known for his crazy sense of humour and was easy to get on with.

Beneath his comical exterior was a man who knew his shit. Outpatient didn't speak much about his past, but when he did it was littered with great escape and covert operation stories. Based on those experiences, he was pedantic about ensuring security operations were run correctly. On this particular evening, he was driving back to the team house with one of the guys when he noticed something strange. Sitting on the side of the road, about 50 metres from the guarded entrance to our street, was a suspicious-looking box.

Outpatient got out of the car and carefully inspected the parcel. He instantly saw that the box had been taped up loosely and had wires protruding from the sides. After he had retreated back to the safety of his armoured vehicle, he got his mate to reverse to a safe distance from the package. He then called the army to report what he'd seen. It was as he was making the call that he noticed a local man appear from out of some nearby bushes and start walking away.

Outpatient jumped out of the vehicle and apprehended the Iraqi. He began questioning him, but the man only spoke in Arabic. Outpatient demanded to see his ID, and the man pulled out a dodgy, obviously fake card. The US army arrived within minutes to speak with Outpatient about the incident. The box turned out to be a dummy IED. The man was arrested and taken away by the military police.

A dummy IED is exactly what it sounds like. It's a fake bomb. The military police believed it had been placed there so that insurgents could watch our response to it. Would we ignore the box? Would we stop and touch it? Would we diffuse it ourselves? The Iraqi man from the bushes was the observer. He was there to record our actions and then report back to his chain of command. The insurgents would then have had the chance to plan an attack on our team based on our actions. These sorts of attacks typically caused the greatest carnage.

Later that night I had nightmares. Over and over I kept dreaming about my son and how I had to protect him. I dreamt about bad people coming into my room and killing me in my sleep. It was all too much. I grabbed my pistol and stuck it under my pillow. After that, I slept like a baby. It's a good thing I managed to get some sleep that night. If I had known what was going to happen the next day, I doubt I would have slept a wink.

Once again I was rostered on at the commissioners' building and once again I was designated the leader. It seemed as though it would be a day like any other in the Green Zone. We picked up our clients from their homes without a hitch. We transported them safely to work, and we discussed their itineraries for the day. Number One had a meeting in the morning, and that was it. I was aware that a visitor was due to arrive later in the morning to speak to our clients, but not much information about it had been released.

All the commissioners' offices were located in the same part of the building. Our security desk was set up near its entrance to ensure that only people with the appropriate level of access could enter. I was sitting at the checkpoint with another teammate when a man named Bob turned up at our station. Bob had once been a member of our team, but had switched to another project within the same company so that he could run building security.

I said hello to him and asked him what was new. He replied that sniffer dogs would be coming through this part of the building shortly, and that I was to let them through without any questions. Obviously something was up. I asked him why they were coming through, but he would not tell me. I asked him if it had something to do with the expected visitor, but he would not answer.

By this stage Bob was pissing me off. If there was someone important visiting my clients, I needed to know about it. If there was a threat against the visitor, I needed to know about it, as my clients would be exposed to the same threat when they met up. Bob was being a prick and wouldn't tell me anything. In fact, he started being quite condescending towards me. I told him to pull his head in and to start working with us as a team. We were both part of the same company and we were both concerned with the safety of our clients within the building. We were the commissioners' close protection team, so we needed to know what he knew.

I was in charge of the clients today. If anything happened to them, it would be my arse that'd be kicked. I told Bob to rack off back to the hole he had crawled out of. I then made some calls and got Cat to come down to sort out the problem. Within half an hour, I had found out what was going on. UK prime minister Tony Blair would be visiting my clients later that morning.

With that knowledge, I made sure that our security protocols were well and truly in place. I briefed each member of my team on the situation and highlighted the importance of secrecy concerning the visit. Number One had to attend a meeting, with 51-50 escorting him, before Blair arrived. I was clear that they were to return as quickly as possible, as Number One was scheduled to welcome the prime minister.

Time ticked on. Some of the UN workers who knew of the visit were getting excited and restless. I looked at my watch: Blair would be here in twenty minutes. I called 51-50 and told him to bring Number One back straightaway. He said that Number One was on stage giving a presentation to an audience. I told 51-50 to slip him a note, telling him it was time to go.

Five minutes later, I still had not heard from 51-50. I called him again. This time he told me that Number One was still on the stage talking, despite being handed a note saying that the prime minister of Britain was arriving shortly. This is the sort of situation that earns a leader their pay packet. I paused for a second before telling 51-50 to escort him off the stage immediately. I told him to be as gentle and inconspicuous as possible, but that he was to remove him from the stage and get him here ASAP.

I said to 50-51 that I would take whatever heat came down as a result of forcing Number One to curtail his speech. What choice did I have? Either I could get him back on time, or let him continue and miss the visit completely, which would have resulted in a loss of face for all the electoral commissioners.

So, imagine if you can, Vin Diesel's doppelganger 'discreetly' escorting the head of the country's electoral commission off a stage. It must have been quite a sight.

Number One was brought back into the office a full minute before the prime minister arrived to shake his hand and exchange a few polite words. Blair's entourage and other VIPs, including high-ranking UN officials and Iraqi government members, had also entered our building. Each VIP was accompanied by their own close protection team, and suddenly our secure area was teeming with visitors. Then my team leaders and even some of the company's head shed turned up. *Word gets around quickly*, I thought. It was typical that they couldn't give a rat's about anything we did on a daily basis with our clients, but the moment a VIP was on the scene, they couldn't keep away.

Tony Blair left as quickly as he'd arrived. Number One confirmed to me that he was not annoyed that he had been pulled away from his speech. In fact, he was grateful. I was pretty pleased with the way things ran despite all the commotion, and the guys I was working with did a superb job.

It was Christmas Eve. The company house had a landline phone that the team were permitted to use to call home, but gaining access to it proved difficult. Every time I made the walk over the house, there would always be a queue of other teams lined up waiting to use it. It was just before Christmas that my team was allocated a mobile phone, which meant I was finally able to talk to Kane, rather than send him emails for his dad to read out. It was wonderful. He was really talkative and very excited about Santa coming. We talked about presents, games and everything he was going to do for the holidays. I wasn't due back home until January, but I planned to spoil him rotten when I returned.

Kane then told me that I was getting a present from Santa too. He told me Santa had a letter for me and that it was going to arrive in time for Christmas. I choked back a sob. Bruce must have sent a card from Kane several weeks ago. The postal service here was slow and unpredictable. It was more likely to arrive early next month. I hoped it came before I left for home.

I missed my little boy so much. I couldn't wait to hold him close. I wanted to play fighting games with him on my bed, just as we used to. I wanted to wrestle him to the ground and tickle him until he cried. After a sad goodbye, I went and had a quiet moment to myself.

*

That night, there was an informal barbecue to celebrate Christmas Eve. The most delicious steaks were cooked on the barbie and a couple of drinks were also consumed. I had to work the next day so I didn't have a late one. During the course of the evening I met Lizard, the country manager from another security firm. I was surprised when, not long into our conversation, he told me he wanted me working for his company.

I was flattered by the job offer, but declined. I still had to finish this contract and did not want to desert the company that gave me my first break in the industry. Lizard understood my reasons, but told me that the offer was good for when I finished up this contract. I wasn't even sure if I'd be taking up another contract at all. Even so, I was amazed at how relieved I felt, knowing that I now had an out if I needed one.

"**M**erry Christmas!" Jeep woke me up early Christmas morning by standing over me and shouting excitedly. I rolled out of bed, grinning. I loved Christmas. Silver came into the room and they both handed me a present. It was a DVD: season two of *Star Trek: The Next Generation*. They knew I was a bit of a Trekkie and loved that series especially. I kissed them both and thanked them profusely. I then pulled out the presents I had bought for them. I had got them a Leatherman set of pocket tools each. I had their call-sign names engraved on them, to give it a personal touch.

After the exchange of presents, I got dressed for work. It was disappointing to be rostered on for Christmas Day, but I had no choice. It was just an ordinary day on the local calendar so it was work as usual. Blade, Wolf, 51-50 and I trudged off to pick up the clients, while the rest of the team geared up for a big Christmas party at the company's headquarters. They were putting on a delicious-sounding lunch, complete with turkey, roast potatoes and alcohol.

It was late afternoon by the time we dropped off the clients at their homes. We arrived back at the team house, but it was deserted. Everyone was still at the other house partying. I had a shower and got changed. As I turned to leave, I noticed there was a letter sitting on my bed. I couldn't believe it: Kane's Christmas letter had arrived. I opened it up and a photo of Kane with Santa fell out onto the floor. *Wow, he has grown!* I wiped a tear from eye as I read his card. I would have to tell Kane that Santa had dropped off the card to me on Christmas Day.

I stuck up the photo on the wall near my bed, and joined the rest of the team at the Christmas party. By the time I arrived, the food was all gone but the alcohol was still flowing freely.

The party was in full swing. Swamp was wearing a gorilla suit, something he had brought with him after returning from leave. He was dancing about, with everyone cheering him on. Baloo had wrapped black plastic bags around his whole body, including his head, and had cut out little holes for his eyes and mouth. He placed a Christmas hat on his head, calling himself 'Mr Christmas Garbage Bag Man'. To me, he looked like Mr Hankey, the Christmas Poo, from *South Park*.

After a few vodka Red Bulls, I stopped drinking. Blade had broken the bad news that we were rostered on at the commissioners' workplace the next day – again. What the hell had happened to the roster system? The same people day in, day out were put on the picquets. We had missed out on the Christmas celebrations. It didn't seem fair that we'd have to work Boxing Day too. I wouldn't let it ruin my night, though.

Jeep pulled me over, wrapped his arms around me drunkenly, and started to serenade me. I joined in with him and together we belted out Evanescence songs. He passed me a beer. I shook my head, telling him that I couldn't drink, as I had to work in the morning.

"No!" Jeep yelled. "I'll get Team America to do it." By that, he meant 51-50, Blade and Wolf. Jeep was American, but he considered himself to be different from those guys. He thought of himself as a cut above them.

"They don't drink anyway. They'll do the job again tomorrow," he said, slurring a bit now. I tried to tell him that I was part of their team and was committed to working in the morning, but Jeep wouldn't hear of it. He wanted me to stay and drink with him. Within five minutes he'd changed the roster and allocated my position to Outpatient.

I felt about two inches tall. Jeep had used his power as the team leader to get his friend – me – out of having to do a job. It was wrong. I couldn't face myself let alone anyone else knowing that my 'connections' in the team were getting me a better ride than others.

I left shortly afterwards and told Outpatient that I would do the job. As it turned out he genuinely wanted to do the shift, but I still felt a bit dirty. I didn't return to the party that night, and, instead, went to bed. Things were getting sticky now, and I wasn't sure how long I could handle it.

Boxing Day arrived and with it a new and exciting task. A small team was needed to fly to Kirkuk by Black Hawk helicopter with some of our clients. The elections were only a month away and things were heating up. The team would be leaving on New Year's Day. I put up my hand for the job straightaway. Dr Evil, Outpatient and Blade put themselves forward too. Our names and passport details were immediately given to the US military. Dr Evil was told he'd been designated leader, and the rest of us would be his team.

We were taken aback. Recently the command staff (including the desk-bound project manager) had been putting themselves on these types of missions at the expense of us worker bees. In fact, a small team was due to leave with a couple of clients for Basra in southern Iraq the following day, and team members had been kicked off the trip so that all the leaders could go. There had been a lot of resentment. Not only did the leaders forgo rotations at the commissioners' workplace, they put themselves on every 'cool guy' mission that came up.

So it was odd that none of them had wanted in on the Kirkuk mission. I later found out the reason: a huge party had been planned for New Year's Eve. Anyone going on the trip to Kirkuk would not be able to drink themself into a stupor the night before.

A couple of days passed, and the leaders returned from their trip to Basra. They'd had a shit of a time. The two clients had not behaved well. When the team arrived in Basra, they had to conduct a quick recon of all the places the clients were going to visit. They needed to know where the meetings would be taking place, what the security requirements were and whether the venues were safe. By the time they got back from the recon, the clients had completely changed their plan. The recon was a wasted task.

Both clients were put up in VIP accommodation at the British Consulate. They were even given a general's room: the best digs in the house. The clients proceeded to drink all the wine in the fridge. Who knows what was in the wine, but it made the clients seriously regress. They jumped on the bed until it broke. They ran up and down the hallway screaming. There was a cake in the general's fridge, which was left over from a birthday party; the clients stuffed their faces with the entire thing. And still they carried on. At one stage, another general burst into their room and yelled at them to behave themselves. The next morning, the clients – and our team – were evicted.

The following night, the clients were forced to sleep in a tent at a British military camp. Unhappy with their new quarters, they complained until they were given a large metal Conex container to sleep in, along with stretcher beds and sleeping-bags. After having their demands met, they promptly fell asleep. The rest of the team was not so lucky. They were ordered by the military to conduct security picquets on the clients all night to ensure they did not get up to any more trouble. It was the price the team had to pay to remain within the safe confines of a military establishment.

The boys were cranky when they got back. Jeep was yelling and cursing about the clients and all the command staff had the shits. The rest of us 'left-over' members had a quiet chuckle to ourselves. To top things off, our Kirkuk trip was postponed by a couple of days, meaning we could have a few drinks on New Year's Eve after all.

On the eve of the mission, I was told to borrow an M-4 weapon from another team member. The promised M-4s had still not arrived, but the company brass wanted us to look as professional as possible during the trip to Kirkuk. Some guys, tired of waiting for the elusive company weapons to arrive, had purchased their own through the local 'weapon network'.

The weapon network was like any other buy and swap system you'd find back home. The only difference was that you were dealing with guns and ammunition. If you needed a specific weapon or weapon attachment, then you'd put the word out, and certain key people from around the Green Zone would source what you needed. AK-47s were very easy to obtain, as they were a dime a dozen in Iraq. Weapons like M-4s and other machine guns were a little more difficult as they had to be imported from other countries – usually the US. The supply and demand of a particular weapon determined its price, and from there you'd barter it down as far as you could.

I was very dubious about using a weapon I had not zeroed or test-fired myself. My AK-47 might have been an antique, but at least I could trust it. I knew it worked, I knew it was zeroed, and I knew it had been well looked after due to my daily cleaning ritual. To use somebody else's weapon was unwise. In the end, I just did as I was told and borrowed the M-4.

I gathered all my kit together. I packed food, water, a borrowed map and a compass. I packed a small medical kit and put my radio on charge. It was only going to be a daytrip and all meals were provided, but I wanted to be prepared for anything. If the chopper went down, I had to have enough food and water to get me by. I'd need my map and compass if I were to get myself back to a safe place.

It was then time to run myself through some M-4 drills. It was not a weapon I had used frequently. I grabbed Spitfire, and he took me through the specifics. I practised over and over again, until I was confident I could use it properly. I thanked Spitfire for helping me out and continued doing some training alone.

The next morning we were up early. Our helicopter was due to fly out at 7.30 a.m. Before then, we had to eat, get our orders, pick up the clients and get to the landing zone. We arrived with plenty of time to spare. As usual, the Black Hawks were delayed, and we had to 'hurry up and wait'. While we hung about, we watched all sorts of people come and go. There were representatives from the

Red Cross, the UN and other aid agencies. Some of them wanted a photo taken with me, as if I were a freak. They wanted to know who I was and what I was doing in Iraq. One woman even wanted me to change over to the company that was providing protection for her. They only employed men and they inhibited her work. She often had to talk to Muslim women in areas that were not safe, but she wasn't allowed to take her male bodyguards with her as they were culturally inappropriate. I thanked her and shook her hand, but explained that her timing was not the best.

The Black Hawk eventually arrived. Then we were off. As the helicopter rose into the air, I felt a deep stirring in the pit of my stomach. I was excited, but also on edge. As we rose into the air, I looked down at the Green Zone. *So that's what Baghdad looks like from up here.*

We began to head out. That's when I saw the real Iraq. We passed over Haifa Street, the deadliest road in Baghdad. It was a no-go zone, unless you had a death wish. There were bombings and killings on an almost daily basis there. In fact, the checkpoint leading to that area from the Green Zone is called Assassin's Gate. Haifa Street was chock-a-block full of people and cars. Traffic was at a standstill, and people were walking all around the marketplace.

I hoped we were high enough to avoid any anti-aircraft missiles, but knew we were not. We were close enough to the ground to clearly see people on their roofs. Gradually, we moved higher into the air and further north until eventually we were out of the city altogether. The terrain then changed to sandy embankments alternating with perfect rows of crops.

As I enjoyed the view, I began to mull over possible 'what ifs'. Could I survive the fall if the Black Hawk went down? If I so, then what? In my head, I began to go over my 'actions on' if anything happened. First aid, security, navigational bearings, water, clients, teammates, and so on. Over and over I played scenarios through my head. Eventually, I gave up and just relaxed into the trip.

It only took about an hour to get to Kirkuk. Landing inside a secure compound, I could see many officials awaiting our arrival. Immediately, we prepared ourselves. When it was safe to disembark from the chopper, the aircrew helped the clients out and we followed close behind. There we were, one hell of a professional-looking team, with all the gear, guns and attitude to match. I had my M-4 by my side and wore a tough-guy expression on my face.

Outpatient had also borrowed an M-4 and was looking pretty slick with all his kit on. As he stepped out of the chopper, he tripped and landed flat on his face. The barrel of his M-4 went straight into the clay landing-zone platform. I helped him up, trying to hide my huge grin, and we continued on. There was another private security team watching our every move, and they had a little chuckle over Outpatient's fall. *There goes our reputation!*

We followed the regional security officer (RSO), who led us to a tent. This was where the meeting would take place with the clients. The RSO informed us that, as this was a secure compound, there was no need to worry about the place being stormed by insurgents.

All visitors attending the meeting would be screened at the entrance to the compound. While the clients were discussing the elections, they would be protected by the integral security arrangements already in place. After dropping off the clients, we were taken to the food hall for a late lunch. This certainly hadn't been one of my what-if scenarios, and I was enjoying myself.

We returned to the tent where the clients were having their meeting, and waited around for them to finish. It was a long day. We didn't end up leaving until midnight. As we flew home, the chill in the air grew more intense. It was nearly two in the morning before we arrived back at the team house.

Dr Evil told us we could sleep in and have the day off. He told us that we'd done a good job and should be proud of ourselves. I was exhausted. It didn't take me long to curl up in my bed and get comfortable. Just before I drifted off, I felt a little jolt of electricity as I remembered: *tomorrow we're getting a new team member*. I couldn't wait. I was finally going to have a partner in crime. We were getting another girl on the team.

I slept in till 8.30 a.m. It felt so good to wake up at my leisure and not be in a rush to get ready for work. I had to rearrange the small corner of the room I slept in to accommodate the new girl. I slept on the bottom bunk so she would need a new mattress for the top bunk. I grabbed some clean sheets and blankets for her bed, and then got Blade to help me bring in another cupboard so she could hang her clothes up. The space was very small and would be even more cramped once she arrived. But it was liveable, and that's what counted in the end.

She arrived just as I was heading out to lunch. She was smaller than me and had the body of an elite athlete: toned and muscled. She had long, straight brown hair, a creamy complexion and seemed very comfortable in her own skin. Her name was Bee, she had a thick Welsh accent and wasn't afraid to say what was on her mind. As soon she arrived she wanted to change the whole bedroom around. She even wanted me to move some of my stuff so that she could place her things there instead.

I wasn't used to people being so pushy and forthright after I'd only known them for five minutes, and I didn't respond well.

Rather than get into a catfight over personal space, I excused myself and took off for lunch. While I ate, I replayed the events in my mind. She was definitely not a shy girl. She lacked tact. Nevertheless, she spoke her mind, which I respected. Would I get on with her? My first impressions were not good. But, like me, she was a minority in this industry, and we had that in common.

I returned after a hearty lunch, thinking that perhaps we had just got off to a bad start. Surely we could put that behind us and try again? She must have been thinking along the very same lines. As soon as we saw each other, we both introduced ourselves again, as though we had never met before. We shook hands and then gave each other a hug. I helped her move her kit into the room and we made a few modifications to room, until we were both happy with the outcome.

Bee's background was impressive: she was an ex–British forces sergeant and a qualified mechanic. While she didn't have any military close protection qualifications, she'd had experience in the area through her last job.

She understood that women had to work much harder than men to be recognised as an equal in the military. So she trained like a demon with her fitness, and had strived to become extremely proficient with her weapon handling, as well as having soaked up all pertinent security information along the way. She was awesome. It was thrilling to be working with another really good operator. She also knew the importance of doing things the right way.

Bee's previous security company was a stickler for policy and procedure – it was like being back in the army, only worse, she said. While they were very good at what they did, her old employer was just too regimented. She was going to get a bloody shock when she realised how this team functioned.

I warned her that she would find herself doing security picquets at the commissioners' workplace most days, and that she'd learn very quickly how the leadership operated. I didn't want to influence her too much, but it was only fair that she be aware of what was going on. She would find out in time what it was like, and could then make her own assessment of the situation.

I was still getting on fairly well with Silver and Jeep, as I couldn't risk getting on the wrong side of them, but I was unhappy with the way things were going with the team. Jeep was all over the place: he was disorganised, longwinded and rambling in his orders, and it seemed he couldn't think straight. Silver was helping him out a lot. In fact, Silver was carrying him.

When Ghost and Merlin came back from leave things got worse. With Ghost's return as the CAT commander, Wolf was discarded like a piece of rubbish and bumped down to being a normal team member again. Wolf was an outsider, and hence had avoided the power trip everyone else was on. When he was in charge, he always did his rotation at the commissioners' workplace, unlike most of the other leaders. Merlin returned as the advanced team leader, while Silver became the permanent assistant project manager.

Stu and Jeep remained as team leaders. Stu was looking at finishing up his rotation earlier than expected. While on leave, he had discovered that he might have cancer. He required medical treatment but wanted to stay on the project to ensure the commissioners were safe during the elections. I gave him full credit for his dedication. It was good to know there was at least one leader on the team who gave a damn about doing a decent job. Stu started to see the leaders as the lazy jagweeds they were. He did his rotations at the commissioners' workplace in a blatant attempt to show up the other leaders' flaws. But they didn't care.

The rest of us noticed, though, and a fissure developed in the team. Over time, that fissure became a crack, and that crack became a canyon. In the end, there were more bloody leaders than workers. For us, it meant more shifts at the commissioners' workplace, and fewer people to do them. How could I stay friends with people who were so flagrantly abusing their position?

Ghost was beginning to piss me off too. He was being outright sleazy towards me. I'd had enough of it. He was as bad as the rest of the leaders. I'd ignored those flaws before, as I was enjoying the feeling of being admired. I was over it now and, in no uncertain terms, I made him aware of it too.

He was not pleased to be told that I wasn't interested. He'd leave me alone and quit being so skeezy around me, but I knew my professional life was going to get harder. I was going on leave shortly and hoped that would give him time to get over it.

I awoke suddenly to the sound of a bomb going off in the distance, a car bomb from the sounds. Just another morning in Baghdad. There was, however, something different about today. I was flying home. Nothing could perturb me. Not the distant bomb, the *pop-pop-pop* of the ensuing firefight or the shit that had gone down at last night's party.

It was the last night in town for Jeep, Silver, Ronin and me before we went on leave. Everyone decided to throw a huge party. The music was loud and the alcohol flowed freely. Bee and I went to bed relatively early. I'd had a couple of drinks but didn't want to go overboard. We still had to do a BIAP trip the next morning in order to get to the airport. There'd be nothing like letting your guard down and dying on your way out of the country: the equivalent of announcing you had 'one more day till retirement'. Besides, I can't consume alcohol and fly anyway. I get motion sickness bad enough without adding alcohol to the problem.

In the early hours, I heard Jeep come into the room, staggering about and cursing under his breath. He managed to get himself into bed. It wasn't long before I heard strange noises coming from his side of the room. They were steady, sort of squishy noises, and gradually they got louder and faster. *Oh my God, he's having a wank!* He had drunkenly got into bed and started tossing himself off.

Perhaps he was too wasted to remember that he shared the room with two women. Perhaps he remembered but didn't care. He groaned. Soon he was snoring away.

It was bloody disgusting, but not that surprising. It's who he was: loud, crass and tactless. Recently, I had heard him on the phone, talking to his girlfriend back in the US. As he was coming home on leave, he demanded that she do all sorts of things for him prior to his return. She had to make sure her nails were done, her hair had to be well groomed, and their house had to be immaculate.

He also told her to make sure she removed her entire 'muff'; he didn't want any pubic hair annoying him when he went down on her. *Romantic stuff.* She was obviously used to his ways because they'd stayed together for many years. Jeep made no secret of the fact that he hated her children from a previous relationship and often spoke about them as though they were devil spawn.

How could someone put up with a lover who treated them as a possession and not a person? I thought of Joe. Maybe I wasn't one to talk. Joe stole from me and lied to me, and I took him back. It took a lot for me to finally break away. I hoped Jeep's girlfriend gained that same strength one day.

At another point during the night – I don't know what time it was – I heard more rustling coming from the other side of the room. I could hear Ghost and Merlin still outside partying, so it couldn't have been anyone else but Jeep. I heard him open up his cupboard. What could he possibly be looking for at this time of night? Well, a toilet, of course! He opened up the cupboard and began to piss into it. It went on for a good minute. At first it was a long, steady stream. Then it began to die down a bit, before starting up again at full power. Would this night ever end?

My car bomb alarm had welcomed me to a new day. I was up, dressed, packed and fed by 7 a.m. I was ready to go. It was a shame no one else was. Ghost, Merlin and Jeep struggled about, swearing and looking for the cleanest clothes they had. Bee was cranky, and I couldn't blame her. She already had difficulties sleeping and the loud partying and noisy boys were taking their toll on her night's rest. I hoped she'd be all right once I'd left. At least only Merlin and Ghost would be left in the room. Perhaps with Jeep gone, things would settle down.

We headed out on the road and, thankfully, the trip was uneventful. Our tactic of keeping a low profile was working for the moment. We had managed to avoid being detected and, hence, attacked while travelling along Route Irish.

We arrived at the airport and it was bedlam. There was no method for collecting tickets, the security was lax, and people were crowding around everywhere. Jeep, Ronin and I already had our tickets, but Silver had yet to purchase his. To buy a ticket, Silver would have to wait in a long line to see a woman sitting at a desk, who had a hardcopy version of the passenger manifold – it was all done manually. The prices of tickets varied depending on whether you were a 'rich' Westerner or a local.

We were well aware of the unspoken 'no seat, no flight' clause that the Iraqi airlines had, but there was no way any of us would be missing this flight out. We were determined to stick together and push our way onto the plane, if it came to it.

After Silver got his ticket, we grabbed our luggage and waited at the boarding gate. When it was time, a bus transported us out onto the tarmac. We loaded our luggage onto the back of the plane ourselves and quickly took our seats. I watched the bus that had transported us to the plane return to the terminal with ten people on board. They missed out today. Perhaps the following day they would be luckier. We then waited a further hour and a half before the finally the plane took off.

As we flew out of Iraq everything felt different. I didn't have to watch my back anymore. Gone were the guns, the armoured vehicles and the tang of testosterone in the air. Out came the fresh, immaculately groomed flight attendants, offering food and refreshments. Sweet perfume infused the air, replacing the smell of sewerage and running generators.

I was heading back to civilisation and a little boy who I loved and missed so much. Soon I would be home, holding Kane in my arms. Soon I would be showering him with kisses and cuddles. We would be talking, playing and laughing. It felt like I had lived a lifetime away from him. Now, I was returning to my son, and to being a mother.

Arriving at the airport in Canberra was unsettling. I'd lived and breathed war for the last three months. This was a place so far removed from what I had experienced that I felt like an alien. All around me people were going about their business: they talked on mobile phones, chatted over cappuccinos and discussed the latest world events.

There I stood, a foreigner in my own country. I was a mother who had wanted to hold her son close but who had grown used to holding the cold, hard barrel of a weapon. I was torn between two worlds and two lives. I was a mother and a nurturer; I was a fighter and protector. How could I be two such different people?

Going down the escalator to the arrivals area, I was anxious. Would my son be frightened by what he saw in my eyes? I could only hope that he would see nothing but the love and adoration of a mother who would do anything for him. And he did. Bruce had brought him to the airport. Kane was there, waiting for me. He rushed up and hugged me with all his might. I rained kisses down on him and pulled him close, then lifted him up and hugged him some more. My boy had not forgotten me, and he still loved me.

Tears filled my eyes as I kissed him all over his face. I thanked Bruce sincerely for bringing Kane to meet me at the airport, nodded and then left. I was back for four weeks. During that time, custody of Kane would revert back to me, with Bruce having Kane once a fortnight at the weekend. After collecting my bags, Kane and I looked for a cab to take us to my aunt's house. She was looking after my car, all my clothes and my personal possessions while I was away. The rest of my stuff was still in storage at my mum's house in Cairns. My mum had broken her leg a few years earlier, so she found the cold Newcastle weather used to make her leg throb incessantly. Shortly before I left for Iraq, she decided to move back to the tropical climate of Cairns in an attempt to escape the pain. We caught a taxi to the other side of Canberra and met up with Aunty Chris.

Kane and I spent a couple of days there, unwinding and playing together. It was as if I had never left. We picked up right where we'd left off and Kane dominated my time, my affections and my attention. We then flew up to Cairns to stay with my mum for two weeks. She was dying to make sure that I was okay and wanted very much to see Kane.

I gave Mum the precious rosary beads Tomahawk's son had made. She put them in her display cabinet for safekeeping. I explained to her that they had been a special gift; they were my protection charm. I wanted her to look after them for me, to ensure that they were not lost or broken. Mum is deeply religious, so I knew she would take good care of the rosary beads for me.

Kane and I spent long, lazy days by the pool and soaked up the sun. I went shopping for gifts and went crazy buying clothes. I bought tops, skirts, dresses and shoes. I snapped up anything that was pink, had sparkles or was ultra-girly. I had been enmeshed in a testosterone-charged environment for so long, I wanted to completely immerse myself in being a girl again. I wore high heels every day, had my nails done and got my hair styled. I lavished gifts on Kane and spoilt him rotten. I took him out to eat at expensive restaurants. I bought into a holiday club, spending thousands of dollars I would not have otherwise spent. I had no regrets. I'd worked hard for my money, and it was time to let loose.

Kane's holidays were coming to an end, and we had to return to Canberra. It was February 2005 and my little boy would soon have his first day of school. I had to be back in time to get him organised. We were staying in a comfortable hotel with a kitchenette, laundry and TV room. I remembered that the Iraqi elections were going ahead. My clients' faces were all over the news, and I proudly rang my mum to tell her I'd been responsible for their safety. The elections seemed to go without too much of a hitch, but they were far from being my top concern. Kane's first day at school was the most important thing as far as I was concerned.

The night before Kane's first day, Bruce rang me to see if his wife, Pamela, could come to watch him go into his new classroom. It was too much. It was like he was pushing me to face her again. I told him no, that I wanted this to be Kane's day. I thought only Bruce and I should be there. Strangely, Bruce accepted what I said. He didn't pressure me or get angry with me. For once, he just listened and left it at that.

The next morning I drove Kane to school. I met up with Bruce in the quadrangle and we did our best to get along so that Kane could just enjoy this special day. Our conversation was strained but civil. We were both nervous about how Kane would deal with school, but he was fine. In fact, we were more worried than he was.

He settled in quite quickly and began to make friends.

After waving at Kane as he went into the classroom, Bruce and I parted ways. He took off for work, and I took off for more retail therapy. At three o'clock I returned to Kane's school to pick him up. As we were driving out of the school gates, I suddenly felt guilty about not including Pamela in Kane's first day. In fact, I had been stewing about it all day.

I no longer felt like I hated her and Bruce. I didn't love Bruce, so there were no more feelings of jealousy and abandonment. I had seen and done so much in the three months I was away that it didn't feel right to keep holding onto my anger. It was redundant.

As I approached a roundabout near their house, I suddenly asked Kane whether I should stop by and make peace with them. Kane said, "I don't know." How could he know? He was just a kid. Stunned by having even asked the question, I kept driving around and around the roundabout until I made a decision. Finally, I indicated left, and turned towards their house.

My palms became really sweaty. My breathing rapidly increased. I could feel my heart beating in my throat. I was unbelievably nervous about taking this step. Perhaps it was Bruce backing down on the phone and respecting my wishes. Or perhaps it was because I felt good inside for the first time in a long while. Whatever it was, I knew I was doing the right thing.

Kane and I got out of the car and walked up to Bruce and Pamela's door. I rang the doorbell. No answer. For a split second, I hoped that no one was home, and that I could turn and quickly walk away. Just as I turned to leave, the door slowly opened and Pamela peered out. I felt sick with nerves. She looked shocked to see me standing at her doorstep.

She was dressed in a pair of tracksuit pants I'd bought Bruce years ago, and an old T-shirt. She was six months pregnant and clearly in the middle of cleaning the house. I apologised for arriving unannounced, but told her I'd felt compelled to see her. I confessed I had even driven around the roundabout several times, trying to decide what to do. I said that I was sorry for not including her in Kane's first day at school, and that I wanted to make peace. She was still a little surprised that I was standing at her front door, but, nevertheless, she invited me inside for a coffee.

She introduced to me her daughter Sonya (who is the same age as Kane), and asked him to show me his room while she brewed a pot of hot coffee. Then, as Kane and Sonya played outside, Pamela and I sat down on her lounge suite and started to talk. Before we both knew it, we were chatting like old friends. We talked about the past, about what we had said and done to each other, and then we shared our insecurities. I couldn't believe I was telling her all the things I had kept bottled up inside me for so long. I couldn't believe she was telling me all the things she had thought and felt over the years as well.

After two coffees, and lots of tears and laughter, we sorted out our issues and a new friendship was born. As I drove home later that afternoon, I felt good about what I had done. I knew it was right. I had got over what had happened in the past and made an effort so that Kane could have a better future.

Life is too short to be absorbed by the things that have hurt you. I have learnt that if you experience intense pain in your life, it is up to you to change the way you feel. You will never get over it if you continue to live your life the same way. If finding inner peace involves making drastic changes to your life, then so be it. Whatever you decide to do, it can't be any worse than the hell you have made for yourself.

When I got home later that evening, Bruce rang to thank me for reaching out to Pamela. He was surprised but happy. The next week and a half passed by, with my friendship with both Bruce and Pamela growing each day. A few days before I was due to return to Iraq, they said they wanted me to stay at their home. They didn't want me paying to stay in a hotel anymore, and invited me to stay in their guest room – and not just during this trip, but whenever I was in Canberra.

I was blown away by their generosity. I didn't want them to feel obligated to have me stay, and I certainly didn't want them to feel awkward while I was in their house. After they had repeatedly told me to stop worrying about things like that, I relented.

Bruce was happy as it meant that he would still see Kane every day, even when I was back from Iraq. Kane was happy as it meant he was able to be with both Mum and Dad at the same time. Pamela was happy as she now had another female friend to gossip, shop and talk with. I was happy as long as everyone else was.

I insisted on paying board, and once again thanked them for their kindness. The three of us talked about what might come after my contract finished up in May. I'd thought about it loads, but I was fairly certain I wanted to return for at least another rotation. My pay packets were hefty: it wouldn't be long before I'd have enough to put down a deposit on a house in Canberra. Bruce and Pamela were very happy to have as much time with Kane as possible.

As Bruce and Kane dropped me off at the airport, I was feeling positive. Kane was a happy and good little boy, who was enjoying making friends and learning new things at school. Bruce and Pamela were becoming close friends, and soon I would have enough money to purchase my own home. I felt renewed and happy about where my life was heading. Work didn't seem like such a big deal anymore. The problems with my team back in Iraq were insignificant, I was certain.

I couldn't have been more wrong.

Some things had changed since I'd been away. Iraq was still in tatters, but a couple of new guys had been hired to join the team. We actually arrived together on the same flight.

The first guy was an Aussie bloke named Camel. He was a short-arse but extremely fit, with a shaven head and a goatee. Camel had been an infantry soldier back in the Australian Army. Since leaving several years before, he had dabbled in "a bit of this and a bit of that", and had been employed as a truckie. He didn't pretend he was an angel, but he wasn't a rough or aggressive bastard either. He had a great Aussie sense of humour and played up to every ocker stereotype you could name.

Cobra, on the other hand, was an ex–British soldier in his early twenties. His mother was Middle Eastern and his father was British. As such, he spoke fluent Arabic and English. Cobra was into everything from buying and selling weapons, to 'acquiring' various items through his contacts in nearby countries. On the drive back to the team house he showed me a gold pistol that he had 'acquired', saying it was possibly from Saddam's own collection. I didn't press him on the details – it seemed better not to know –

and just admired the weapon for its beauty.

As soon as I arrived back at the team house, Bee pulled me aside. She explained that we had a new room, one separate from Ghost and Merlin. She told me that the partying was out of control and she was struggling to sleep at night. The boys were making so much noise and carrying on like such drunken idiots it was affecting her sleep.

The guys weren't just partying til 10 or 11 p.m. and then going to sleep; they were carrying on all night, playing loud music and running amok. Bee said she had been half crazed from lack of sleep. So she pushed and pushed until she was finally permitted to relocate to a quieter room. Jeep, Silver and Ronin were due back the following day. If the partying was off the leash now, it would only get worse with Jeep back in town.

Most of the American guys were on leave. There were fewer 'good guys' for Bee and me to talk to. In their absence, the backstabbing went up a notch. Then I heard that 50-51 wouldn't be returning. Ghost boasted that he had managed to get him fired – not because 50-51 was incompetent or unable to do his job, but because Ghost didn't like him. I realised then just how arrogant and unprofessional Ghost really was. Clearly, it was dangerous to cross him.

I was glad Bee and I had switched rooms. Ghost was a jerk, Merlin was becoming a cocky bastard, and Jeep was a total slob. Silver was competent at his job, but more and more he was siding with Jeep and the other leaders, and not the team. He was too close to them. They were influencing his decision-making and the team was suffering as a result. He was a textbook example of why a leader needed to maintain distance from his staff and not become caught up in the power of the 'boys club'.

The pattern was well and truly fixed now: each night the leaders would stay up late, drinking and carousing; while they nursed their hangovers the next morning, the rest of us continued with our rotations at the commissioners' workplace. A week after my return, I'd had it. I refused to be a commander at the commissioners' workplace unless I was paid the appropriate wage. All I achieved was goading the leaders into turning up to the Convention Center a couple of times, before things reverted to the way they were.

They never appointed me as leader again, and ended up roping in poor old Camel to take on the job. He had been moved into their room and was then given the leadership task. He wasn't going to say no. He had only just arrived and was keeping his mouth shut. I recognised the impulse. He took over as the leader – a guy with no close protection experience at all, who had been in the country a week.

Around that time my life turned into a bloody soap opera. Feeling pretty low and despondent, I entered into a relationship with one of the guys on my team. It was an unwritten rule that you don't fraternise with anyone else on your team, but I was over it. I didn't care about the rules. The leaders never followed them; why should I?

Eagle and I started seeing each other in secret. Eagle was a clean-cut, 'All American' guy on my team. He was a little shorter than me and had a heart of gold. He was always very considerate towards me and made the long days at the Convention Center bearable, but it wasn't long before my professionalism got the better of me. I knew it was wrong and I realised I did not want to lower my standards just because my leaders were below par. So I sat down one morning and wrote a letter to the head of the company: I brought everything out into the open, revealing my relationship and requesting that he either transfer me to another project, or accept my resignation.

The response was not what I had expected. My reputation counterweighed any complaints that my team leaders might have made about me, and the company was keen to keep me employed. It was decided that I would continue to work on the contract, and that Eagle might be moved to another project some time down the line. The company director, Simon, stated that just because I had entered into a relationship with a colleague did not mean my employment had to be terminated. "These things happen," he said to Silver. Silver was surprised by the company's attitude – as was I – but we were both happy with the response. I was still a valued member of the team, as far as Silver was concerned.

Ghost, however, was furious. He was still fuming from my rejection of his advances and had been convinced that I would be sacked. He was wrong, and that only fuelled his hatred of me.

Our team were finally given new weapons: two Minimi machine guns. Only a few of us on the team were qualified to use them – Swamp, Ronin, Cobra and me – as no one else had used one before. Cobra and Ronin were told to go out and test the weapons to make sure they were in good working order.

Cobra asked me if I'd help to zero the Minimis so that his day would not drag on too long. It would be good and worthwhile training for me, I reasoned, especially as I was going to be carrying the weapon on BIAP trips. It had been a while since I'd fired a Minimi and I spent some time re-familiarising myself with the weapon's drills. I went through my immediate stoppage drills, my weapon operation drills and basic firing positions before I headed down to the military range with Ronin and Cobra.

My weapon-handling skills were a bit rusty but, by lunchtime, they were back under control. We did discover one important thing: the weapons were faulty. They fired as we cocked them. I didn't know whether it was a problem with the hardware that needed to be fixed by an armourer, or if a change in ammunition would do the trick. I'm no expert; I just fire the things. I thanked Ronin and Cobra for taking me down there with them, and then we returned to the team house.

The guys back at the house got ready to go to lunch. I wasn't very hungry and decided to leave them to it. Before leaving, Cobra came over to me to have a quiet word. He said that someone in the house thought I should not have gone to the range to fire the Minimi. I asked him who could possibly be upset about that. He replied that he didn't know but that he was going to find out.

I sat in my room, confused. Who would bitch about my going to the range and zeroing a weapon? It was a rare day: I wasn't rostered on at the commissioners' workplace, and there weren't any other tasks for me to complete here. I hadn't ducked doing any work. If I hadn't been at the range, I would have just been sitting in my room watching *Star Trek* DVDs. It made no sense at all.

I went to see Ronin. He had moved into Merlin and Ghost's room, along with Camel, when Bee had moved us out. I asked him if there had been any problems this morning at the range. He responded that there had been no problems; it had been a great help. I shrugged and turned to leave.

Then I noticed Ghost in the corner of the room. He was on his laptop as always, checking out women's online dating profiles. He lowered his screen, looked into my eyes, and announced that *he* had a problem with my going to the range. I looked at him incredulously. Ghost shut his laptop and stood up. He told me that I shouldn't have gone to the range: I was supposed to stay in the house. I was sure I must have misheard him.

I told him that I'd been asked to help zero the Minimis, as I was one of only a few people qualified to use the weapon. I had nothing else to do except watch DVDs. I couldn't see the issue.

"I don't give a fuck," Ghost replied. "You shouldn't have gone."

"Sorry?" I couldn't get my head around what was happening.

"You heard me. You shouldn't have gone. And if you don't like the rules, then quit."

"Let me get this straight," I retorted. "If I don't agree with you that I should have been sitting in my bedroom, watching DVDs for five hours, instead of training and zeroing a machine gun, then I should quit?"

"Yes," he replied vehemently.

That's when I twigged. Ghost had decided he wanted me off the team; this was his unsophisticated method for making it happen.

I let loose a volley of swear words and stormed out of his room, slamming the door shut behind me. The windows shuddered and sound echoed throughout the house. I walked outside the front door and into the front yard. Then I backed into the side alley and bawled my eyes out.

Ghost couldn't see past the fact he'd been slighted, and now he hated me. Leaders are supposed to get on with job, regardless of whether they like their staff personally. They are supposed to rise above petty likes and dislikes, and just play to their team members' strengths. Ghost didn't give a shit. He just wanted to hurt and then fire the people he didn't like. He'd done it with 51-50, he was trying to do it to the other Americans, and now he was doing it to me.

I used a tissue to wipe my eyes. I wouldn't make it easy for him, the arsehole. I'd never quit before, and I wasn't going to start now. If he wanted to fire me, he'd have to work hard to do it.

Having seen out Iraq's first elections, Stu had decided to leave the project to receive medical treatment. I never saw him again. Baloo and Dr Evil came back from leave in mid March, and their return shook things up a bit. Silver remained as the assistant project manager, Jeep the overall team leader, Merlin the advanced leader, Ghost the CAT commander, but now Dr Evil would be the main body commander.

Dr Evil was like a breath of fresh air. We were on the same page on many issues. He agreed that all the leaders should be doing their time at the commissioners' workplace. He agreed that team members should not be in charge of the commissioners' movements around the Green Zone, nor should they be taking up unpaid leadership positions. Immediately, Merlin and Ghost found themselves doing their rotations at the commissioners' workplace again. It was satisfying to see them pulling their weight, but, as usual, it didn't last long. Soon it was only Dr Evil doing the rotations, while the other two skived off.

*

I decided to end my relationship with Eagle. He was a nice person, and I realised I was not being fair to him. He wanted me to quit working in Iraq and move to America with him. There was no way that would happen: my son was in Australia. Rather than risk all that hurt in the future, I called it quits. I felt so bad for hurting him; he was an absolute gentleman. Life went on. Things were sticky between us personally, but we still remained professional. We both had jobs to do and we had to push aside our feelings.

Cobra was a 'networker'. He knew people. He knew how to get things, and he made a lot of money doing it. After you'd told Cobra what you wanted, he would speak to his contacts, and make deals with them. He'd then come back to you to let you know what you had to hand over in order to get the item. It might be money or it might be something else you had; it might even be a favour. Whatever it was, he would deliver it to the interested party, and then return with the item. Somehow he would extract a profit from both parties, and that was how he made extra money in Iraq.

At first I didn't realise how much Cobra was into this kind of 'bartering system'. As his phone began to ring on a regular basis, followed by long talks behind closed doors, I realised something was going on. He'd take off for ages in a vehicle, then come back, looking like the cat that had caught the mouse. *Another successful deal!*

A BIAP trip was organised to take Cobra out to the military airport. He was going to Kuwait to pick up some supplies. Logistics was a big problem for private security companies in Iraq at that time. It was not easy to ensure that the supplies you purchased arrived. There would be delays in orders, problems with customs from the sending country, and the pilfering of equipment when it made it into Iraq. Cobra spoke Arabic and found he could get whatever the company required. He would leave on weekend 'shopping expeditions', then return some time later with everything that had been on the company's wish list. This made him a favourite at the company's headquarters.

A few days later, six of us sat in the lounge room, waiting. There was Mr Happy, the Irishman who had shared a room with Merlin, Ghost and Jeep, until they gave him so much shit he had to move. There were Spitfire and Bee, a South African named Horse, another Brit named Buster, and me. We were six little rejects awaiting our orders for the day.

Mr Happy had been selected as the team leader for the day and told he was to write mission orders for a BIAP trip. We were told that none of the other team leaders would be going with us, and that we were on our own. There had been a huge party the night before, and most of the team leaders were hung-over and asleep in their beds.

Mr Happy gave us orders. I was the designated driver of an armoured BMW; Bee would drive the soft-skinned CAT wagon, which after extensive repairs was now ready for use again. Mr Happy was to be my vehicle commander, and Horse my rear shooter. Spitfire and Buster would jump into the CAT wagon to be Bee's shooters.

Ghost walked past and interjected: he said that we were expected to travel at 160 kilometres an hour along Route Irish. I told Mr Happy at the end of the orders that there was no way in hell I was going to do that. I was not normally employed as a driver and did not know where all the potholes and IED craters were on that road. If I hit one of them at those speeds, I'd probably kill us all, especially considering how slippery the roads were after a week of heavy rain. Not only that, but if a US army convoy or other PSD team came on us travelling at that speed, it was likely they would shoot us dead, assuming we were insurgents.

Never had we been ordered to drive at that speed. It was crazy. Usually we coasted at about 100 kilometres an hour. Mr Happy told me to ignore Ghost and stick to the speed he'd mentioned in orders. It was time to leave.

We were in two vehicles: six contractors and no company-sanctioned leaders. There was no reaction force or CAT to come to our aid if we got into trouble. We were on our own. Rain began to pour as I made my way through the Green Zone checkpoint. I gradually stepped on the pedal and began to accelerate down Route Irish. I was dodging some potholes and flying straight over the top of others. I couldn't miss them all.

Bee kept up with me in the CAT wagon, pushing the van's engine to its limits. After showing our IDs and clearing our weapons at the Camp Victory checkpoint, we drove to the military airbase. The roads were muddy and completely swamped with water in parts. It was a long, slow trip, and the beat-up old BMW I drove struggled to get through the mud.

Eventually, we arrived at the airbase to find it was flooded. We parked the cars and got out to take a look around. In order to get to the airport control rooms, we had to wade through thigh-high water. Mr Happy and I half swum up to one of the people in charge to ask them when the military aircraft Cobra was on would arrive. We were told that it had been diverted to Basra and would be delayed for a few hours.

We returned to the vehicles to let the other guys know. Mr Happy decided that the team should weather the storm at the huge

American PX store while he waited for the aircraft. Sitting in the BMW, I turned the key in the ignition. Nothing happened. I tried it again. Still nothing. My car had bitten the dust. One by one, each member of team tried to start the engine, but they all failed.

It was dead. To this day, I don't know what happened to the car, but it was so ancient it could have been any one of myriad problems. Mr Happy was beginning to get stressed. I could see it in his eyes. I suggested he ring the team leaders to tell them what had happened. I hoped they would send a recovery team to pick up the rest of us. As for the vehicle, until they came up with a proper recovery plan, it should remain where it was.

Mr Happy told us to go off to the PX store while he made some phone calls. We were to pick up some lunch for him from Burger King, while we were there. On the way to the PX, I thought about all that was happening. Everything about this trip was wrong. Why had we been sent out here without proper team leaders, without a full team, and without the usual third vehicle?

We picked up some shopping, grabbed Mr Happy's lunch, and made for the military airbase. Mr Happy was not living up to his name. His phone kept cutting out, making communication difficult. Cobra's plane had been delayed once again, and it now looked to be another two hours before it would arrive. Mr Happy blew out a mouthful of air before he hit us with the real bombshell.

No one was coming to get us. Mr Happy told us that we were to remain in place and continue to try and start the vehicle. Apparently, the team leaders were going apeshit back at the team house. Ghost assumed that I must have done something to disable the vehicle. Once again, he was just looking for a reason to have a go at me. Mr Happy, as the designated team leader, and a passenger in my vehicle, told Ghost to settle down. I had not done anything wrong to the vehicle; the engine had simply just refused to turn over.

Two hours later, we were finally informed that the aircraft would not arrive at all, as it was far too wet and muddy to land here. Mr Happy was back on the phone, informing Jeep of the situation. I could see Mr Happy's jaw tense as he listened on the phone. He hung up, shaking his head: the plan was that we would all jump into the CAT wagon and head home in that one soft-skinned vehicle.

This was lunacy. If we were hit on the road, then every one of us would die. Who was going to make the phone call for help if we got into trouble? I wouldn't be able to phone for help if I had been hit and was lying in a pool of blood in the back of the van. No one else would, either, as they would all be dead or dying in the back of the van next to me. I was really fired up.

Bee started the wagon, and we all piled in. I took a photo of us all, a memento of what we were about to do. Bee made a phone call to her boyfriend and told him what was going on. He worked with Lizard's security company and they had access to 'mobile assets'. He'd ensure that there was some protection for us out on the road. So we were reduced to looking to another company, rather than to our team leaders, for support.

Bee drove as though our lives depended on it, which they did. Twelve years as an army mechanic, combined with having grown up on a farm, made Bee a gutsy driver. I would not have felt safer with anyone else behind the wheel. She drove like a hellcat, and got us back safely to the Green Zone.

We all got out of the vehicle, silent and seething. I walked into the house, threw my weapon and webbing on my bed, and stormed straight into Silver's office. Once inside, I told Jeep and Merlin, who were hanging about like the shiftless pricks they were, to leave. I slammed the door shut behind them.

I could put up with a lot of crap, but I drew the line at my leaders sending my team and me out on a suicide mission.

I unleashed on Silver. I told him that Ghost, Merlin and Jeep had no right to send us on that trip. No one had ever been sent out like that before. How dare none of the 'paid' team leaders go on that trip? How dare they accuse me of breaking the vehicle on purpose? How dare they send us back to the Green Zone in only one soft-skinned vehicle, and deny us another security vehicle for protection?

They were our leaders. It was their responsibility to ensure the security and safety of all their team members. They didn't have to like us, but they had to at least try not to actively kill us. I told Silver there was no way I was ever going out on a Red Zone trip organised by those leaders again. I told him I was no longer willing to put my life in jeopardy for those guys. They were useless and negligent and playing with our lives – and I'd had enough.

We were supposed to be security experts. We were supposed to be the ones who avoided risks. That was our job, and the bloody leaders weren't doing theirs well enough. The result was that they were putting us at risk. I didn't think they were doing it on purpose; they just couldn't have cared less about us. Their problem was that they simply didn't take their jobs seriously. Any leader with proper training understands the importance of good leadership on a team. Except we weren't a team right now; we were insurgent bait.

With that, I turned and left. I poured myself a full glass of rum and sculled it down. I returned to my room and proceeded to go off my nut.

Silver came into my room a little while later and sat down on my bed. He apologised and said he didn't know what Jeep, Ghost and Merlin had been thinking when they sent us out. He told me it was wrong and that it wouldn't happen again. I accepted his apology, but I was adamant that I would never work with them again.

Silver considered my comments and made me an offer. He knew I was an asset to the team and didn't want to see me leave. He asked me if I would consider working for the team in a different capacity, whether I would take on an administration role. None of the other team leaders could make heads or tails of the normal Word and Excel spreadsheets that had to be completed daily. Silver asked me if I would take on this role for him, even sweetening the deal with an extra $50 a day. I would still be required to do security rotations at the commissioners' workplace, but he promised I would not be sent out on the road again with those leaders.

I considered his deal and then accepted. As long as I didn't have to work with Ghost, Merlin and Jeep, I would be okay. I felt for everyone else on the team, though. It was their lives that those 'leaders' would be taking chances with.

Over the next few days, I immersed myself in the administration side of the project. I still did my security rotations at the commissioners' workplace, but away from that environment, I sat in front of my computer. I organised leave rotation plans, coordinated leave travel arrangements, and updated next-of-kin registers. I compiled manning status reports (which detailed what tasks each team member was performing for the day), updated budget spreadsheets, typed out invoices, and most importantly, sorted out everyone's pay sheets.

I saw better ways of articulating information, and made the appropriate changes. Silver was extremely happy, as the team's administration was finally being done competently and without problems. He didn't have to worry about double-checking my work, as he knew I could manoeuvre my way around a computer. This kind of administration was Mickey Mouse stuff compared to what I had done in my military career.

Things cruised along quietly for a while. Cobra put the hard word on me, but at first I wasn't sure whether I wanted to have a relationship with someone twelve years my junior. Then, as life on the project was currently pretty shitty, I thought, *What the hell?* Technically, I wasn't part of the team anymore; I was administration. Cobra wasn't technically part of our team either, although he did go on BIAP trips when needed. Cobra was chiefly working as an instructor. He was employed by our company to train locals in close personal protection. It was envisaged that the Iraqi team would take over from us in a few months' time, when our contract ended.

I was happy to have a bit of a fling: Cobra was young and very good-looking. Perhaps it was a matter of the band playing as the *Titanic* sunk, I don't know. The whole team was so dysfunctional, it was only a matter of time until it all collapsed. I thought I would take my fun where I could find it. And it gave Ghost the shits, which was gratifying.

Soon another client trip was organised for the team. As I was no longer working for the leaders on those kinds of trips, I didn't even bother turning up to the orders group. I knew they were heading out into God knows what part of the country and that they were going by vehicle. It was more bloody madness, as far as I was concerned. *Since when do we drive our clients into the middle of Iraq?* I wondered. We were not convoy escorts – guys with big pay packets but short life expectancy – we were security experts!

Any kind of reasonable security assessment would have told them it was far too risky to drive through Iraq with a tier-one target on board. We had US military assets at our disposal. We had aircraft, armoured vehicles and soldiers. If this trip was important, why weren't those assets used? Instead, they decided to use one armoured SUV (to carry the client), and two soft-skinned SUVs, even though the company had access to a few armoured SUVs.

Ghost was running the team, and it wasn't clear why he chose such a careless and dangerous method for transporting our clients. Would they and the rest of the team be safe? For some reason, I was really worried about Tomahawk. I couldn't get the thought of him out of my head.

The team took off that morning. I wanted to send Tomahawk a text message to make sure he was okay, but I did not want to distract him from his duties. He was their rear gunner; he needed to remain alert throughout the trip. Later that night we heard that they had made it safely. I heaved a sigh of relief. *They were okay*. Even so, I worried incessantly the following day, the whole time they were making their return journey.

I ate my way through that morning, waiting for the team to make it back to the Green Zone. Chicken noodle soup and Oreo biscuits helped the time to pass more quickly. Late in the afternoon, I heard them come through the front door. I ran downstairs and gave Tomahawk a quick hug. I don't know why it was just him I was concerned about, as it was good to see all their faces. Then Ghost came in, strutting like a warrior, and commenced his stories of 'war and honour'.

Ghost told everyone that the trip had gone well, with no signs of insurgent activity. *Of course bloody not. If there were, you'd all be dead.* He told us how when they arrived at the compound at the end of the trip, the other security teams said they thought they were crazy. They had told Ghost it was suicide to travel the way that they had. Ghost didn't take that as a criticism; he took it as a compliment. He was brave. He had done something every other security team would avoid at all costs. He was a tough and courageous team leader, as he had made the trip and survived. What a wonderful story this would make: the time when he went driving through Iraq in soft-skinned vehicles, getting his tier-one target to his meeting. He saw it as a glory story. Ghost couldn't see it for what it was: a textbook example of poor tactical decision-making, poor leadership, and poor fucking judgment.

I nearly made myself sick listening to his crap. In the end, I walked away. I couldn't listen to him spinning his yarn, when his actions could have cost his team their lives. What a fucking joke! And I was part of this joke. In fact, I was in charge of paying these jerks. I was no better. I had twenty days left on my contract. I hoped I could last the distance.

My time on the project was almost up. I knew the end was coming. Ghost was not happy about my new relationship with Cobra, but that was just the excuse he was using to get rid of me. I was clashing with the leaders on a regular basis. I had made it my business to question everything they did. I couldn't rest until I had exposed them for what they were – frauds.

During my first rotation in Iraq, I had remained silent and kept my views to myself. This time around, I couldn't watch what was happening and not say anything – even if it meant losing my job. I was an ex–officer of the Australian Army, and a person who believed in doing the right thing. So I questioned them whenever they left themselves open for an attack, and, because that occurred frequently, they soon learnt to despise my sharp tongue.

To sack someone for opening their mouth is not enough. I wasn't the only person complaining about the way the team was being run. Outpatient wrote a letter to the company manager detailing the 'extreme leadership failures' within our team, and requested they take action to remedy the situation immediately. Nothing was done. Dr Evil and Baloo had taken a stand, as had

Wolf and Bee. Even Cobra had tried to tell the leaders, as a friend, that they were being too reckless, but they wouldn't listen. If they started dumping everyone who was talking shit about them, there would be no one left. Ghost needed a really good reason that would see me gone, and he didn't wait long to make his move.

One day a letter appeared on the notice board. The company had 'decided' that no one was allowed to have a relationship with another company member. Any breach would result in the termination of those people's contracts. It was quite clear to me that this was a measure directed at me in particular, and that Ghost had been the one to orchestrate it. Not two months before, the company director himself had shrugged and said, "These things happen," when I tried to resign after coming clean about my relationship with Eagle. This same company employed a husband-and-wife team. I didn't buy that this sudden about-face hadn't had an instigator.

So, there I was, sitting in the country manager's office with Ghost off in a corner looking like Gollum from *The Lord of the Rings*. The country manager told me to resign or else I'd be sacked. Resigning would mean that the company could sue me for breach of contract if I picked up employment with another PSD. Getting sacked would mean a tarnished reputation, but I would still be able to pick up work in Baghdad without risk of legal action. Should I save face (and my reputation) and resign my position, or tell them to fuck off and let them sack me?

I began to think back over my time in the team. I thought back to the moment I overheard Jeep, Ghost and Merlin bitching about 'certain' team members. I heard them say, "The only team members we have problems with are those who are qualified." For once, they were right. Only qualified people stood up to them because we knew what we were talking about. I was sick of it all.

After considering the country manager's option for maybe thirty seconds, I told him they could sack me. In addition, I'd require a letter stating the reasons for my termination. And that was it. I turned and walked out of the office.

I walked back to the team house, where I began to pack up my things. I would be leaving in the next day or two. As soon as I could get a flight out of the country, I would be gone. I went back to my room and told Bee what had gone down, as I put all my gear into a couple of large plastic trunks. Bee was upset that I was going and could not believe what had happened. She told me that she'd just spoken to Cobra: he had not been sacked. He had not even had a rap over the knuckles. That sealed it: it had been a stitch-up.

Bee knew I was not leaving because of a relationship with another guy in the company. This was all about someone speaking out. I chose to speak my mind because it was the right thing to do. I felt satisfied that I had done everything in my power to make things right on the team. I used my friendship with the leaders to offer advice, but they didn't want it. I bucked the system and spoke aggressively to them, and still it had no effect. They had sent me and my teammates out on suicide missions, and they still didn't understand they were messing with people's lives.

I was booked to fly home the following day, and had not yet made any firm plan about coming back to Iraq. There was more to discuss with Bruce about Kane's care. Now that the company had terminated my contract, I was no longer bound by the clause that prohibited me from finding work somewhere else. I could walk across to Lizard's company tomorrow if I chose to. I had options. My career wasn't over just yet.

If they thought they had won by firing me, they were mistaken. Emotionally, no one could hurt me. I'd been there and done that. I'd already endured the worst pain of my life when my relationship with Bruce broke down and my dream of living together as a family of three died. If sacking me for caring about my professionalism and the lives of my teammates was their best move, then they were wasting their time.

Whether I came back tomorrow, or in a month's time, it didn't matter. I was coming back, and I was determined to do better with my next team. As it turned out, I didn't have a choice about leaving the next morning; the decision was made for me.

I awoke early. The sun was barely up and the air still had a chill in it. I couldn't sleep so much was running through my mind.

I thought about all the crap I had put up with and everything I had endured. It had all come to an end. I would fly home that day to see Kane. I needed to be with him. He was my reason for living and working each day. I needed to go home and feel like a normal person again. After some relaxation, I would be in a better state to continue working.

After a few phone calls the previous evening, I had made up my mind that I was going to work for Lizard. The company he worked for was huge. They had many assets, their logistical chain was good and they employed highly qualified personnel. Each member was required to complete an intensive training course and work experience program prior to their working on a security detail.

Lizard's company didn't normally hire women for security roles, nor did they hire many Aussies. I would be breaking down barriers just by joining it, and I was proud to do so. I'd go home on leave, and then return in a month or two to begin working on one of their projects. I was happy with the plan I had mapped out.

The team was scheduled to drive me to the airport at 10 a.m. I still had a few hours before they got out of bed. Once again, there had been a heavy drinking session the previous night, so I didn't expect to see anyone about for a while. I made myself a mug of coffee and sat down in the lounge room to think about things. As I drank my coffee, I began to feel really good. I was excited about going home to Kane, and I was relieved that my time with the company was finally over. I drained the last drops of coffee, then poured myself another. I just wanted to relax and savour the moment.

I sat back down on the lounge chair and went to take a sip. As I brought the mug up to my mouth, coffee spilt, burning my bottom lip. Surprised by the sudden onset of pain, I jumped. My hand jerked upwards, causing the hot liquid to tip out of the mug and onto my pants.

The scalding-hot coffee penetrated my trousers through to my skin. I screamed out in pain as the burning liquid leaked through my underwear. The coffee mug fell out of hand and shattered into a million pieces as it hit the ground. I ran up to my room, yelling to Bee that I had burnt myself. She jumped out of bed as I quickly undressed.

"Get my burns kit out. Get my burns kit out," I said. When I was seventeen, I spilt boiling-hot water over my leg on the night of my debutante ball. I understood how bad a burn could become if it was left unattended, so I made sure to always carry a burns pack in my personal first-aid kit. I jumped into the shower, grabbed the nozzle and directed soothing cold water onto my wound. I returned to the room, lay down on my bed, and then awkwardly placed the burns treatment pads onto my private parts.

I didn't have enough to cover the whole area, but the important bits were taken care of. I told Bee that there was no way I could get on a plane today. I'd have to go to the military hospital

(CSH, pronounced 'cash') to have the injury looked at. Even though it wasn't a severe burn, it was in a very sensitive area. The burns kit provided relief, but I was still in pain. I was aching and emotionally drained. *Just when I thought I was going home ...*

As I lay on my bed, Bee went downstairs to let the leaders know what had happened. Instantly, Ghost demanded to see how bad the wound was. I told Bee to tell him to fuck off. There was no way in hell I was going to let him take a look at my burn. I needed to see proper medics. I was throbbing down below and knew the pain would only get worse if I sat on a plane for the next twenty hours. My wound had to be dressed properly, and some painkillers wouldn't go astray either. Bee came back into the room with an angry look on her face. She told me that downstairs the leaders were flipping out.

Crazy things were happening because the leaders had no ability to deal with a change in plans. They were losing it because my injury meant they would not be leaving on time. Jeep even went so far as to accuse me of staging the whole thing so that I could remain in the country longer, as that would mean the company had to continue paying me. I was incredulous. I wanted to go home. I wanted to see my son. Why would I want to delay that? Jeep was off his tree. I thought for sure he must have taken some full-on drugs the previous night because he was out of control. Both Merlin and Silver were out of the country on leave, and Jeep was not coping with all the extra duties.

Bee couldn't take me to the CSH that morning. She had to get ready for the BIAP trip she was making with the team. In fact, no one could drive me. Or should I say, no one was allowed to drive me to the CSH. Instead, I was ordered to drive myself. Tomahawk offered to give me a lift, but I told him no. I didn't want him to get in trouble for my sake.

Tomahawk pulled me aside before I left and told me that I would be okay. He told me to be strong and to forget about what was going on with the leaders. He gave me hug and then said goodbye. I grabbed a set of keys and carefully got into a vehicle. I drove off to the CSH with tears flowing down my face. I was hurting emotionally and physically. These men who had once been my friends had sent an injured member of their team, alone and without a weapon for protection, to the CSH. I felt abandoned.

I drove slowly along the road, as the speed limit near the CSH was only 10 kilometres an hour. Just as I passed the hospital entrance, an explosion erupted from my vehicle. I can still feel the vibrations in my hands to this day. I lost steering power and crashed into a concrete barrier near the road. My first thought was that my vehicle had been hit with an IED. I furiously looked around, waiting for the onset of small-arms weapon fire. But there was none. The car was not on fire. It was just not moving. I tried to start the engine, but nothing happened.

A US soldier standing guard outside the CSH came over to see if I was okay. He couldn't understand what had happened either. One minute I had been driving along the road, and the next my vehicle had crashed into a cement blast wall. *What the hell was going on?* My day was getting crazier by the minute.

I rang Bee to let her know what had happened and telling her I needed assistance to recover the vehicle. I was blocking traffic along the road, and the engine was stuffed. Being the team's resident mechanic, Bee came down to take a look at the car. She brought Baloo and Dr Evil with her so that they could help to tow the vehicle away. They began to look over the vehicle: there was nothing wrong with it externally, except that the front right-hand tyre was ruined from hitting the wall. They opened up the hood and tried to start the engine. Once again, it would not turn over.

In the end, they put it down to bad fuel. The bad fuel must have blown the engine, which caused me to lose steering control. It was lucky I was only going at a snail's pace. Dr Evil and Baloo assured me that everything would be okay; they'd tell the leaders that the vehicle had malfunctioned and caused the accident.

Jeep and Ghost wouldn't believe them. To my humiliation, they declared me a 'suicide risk'. They wanted a full medical report from the doctor too, as they were convinced I was faking my burns injury to avoid leaving the country. Bee was pulled off the BIAP trip and told to stay with me, in case I did anything 'silly'. I was livid by this stage. My private parts were hurting and the leaders were labelling me suicidal. They had finally gone too far.

Days later, when Bee had a better chance to look at my crashed vehicle, she found that bad fuel was not what had caused the accident. Whoever had checked the air filter when the vehicle was last serviced had not put the coupling back on correctly. The coupling was put under pressure when I was driving around. This pressure culminated in what sounded like an explosion, as the coupling popped off. This, in turn, cut out the engine and disabled the steering wheel. By that stage, so much had transpired that the car was the least of my worries. Even so, it was good to have an explanation.

I hobbled into the CSH and was seen by a military nurse. She looked at my wound and told me that the burns treatment I used had assisted me tremendously. There was a small section not covered by the gauze that had blistered slightly, but, apart from that, I was doing okay. She gave me some painkillers, dressed my wound, and then sent me on my way. The nurse handed me my medical forms and I took off with Bee.

Bee dropped me off at the country manager's house as I had some unfinished business with him. This was it. I was not going to leave until I'd said my bit and given it to him straight. Those leaders were out of their fucking minds, and it was his duty to put an end to what was going on.

I strode into the country manager's office to find another man sitting at his desk. He explained that the manager was out of the country and that he was the acting country manager (Acting CM). Acting or no, he was going to hear some serious shit from me. I slapped my medical slip on his desk and told him that it was my proof that I had burnt myself earlier. I was not 'faking an injury', as had been insinuated by Ghost and Jeep.

The Acting CM had only a basic idea of what was going on between the team leaders and me. So I told him everything: the kamikaze missions, the cocaine use, the bullying and intimidation, the gross irresponsibility and dangerous risk-taking. I had been sacked for having a relationship, while the other party didn't get so much as a dressing-down. I'd had to fight to be given the same opportunities as the men I worked with, despite my being more experienced and better qualified than them. So much for being treated the same as my male counterparts, so much for the 'equal workplace' the company boasted that it had.

I grew weary. Nothing was going to change, no matter what I said. This man was only here for a few days; what could he do? I looked at him solemnly, and then said my final words to him. I told him that the leaders on this project were dangerous and that they were going to get members of the team killed.

The Acting CM drew in a long breath. He had only been with the company for a couple of weeks, and was blown away by what I had said. He was an ex–British forces high-ranking officer. He told me that everything I'd said had merit, and was most likely true. He said, "Things happen for a reason, and you have now found yourself unable to change the consequences of speaking up. It has happened to me, and, ultimately, it ended my military career."

The Acting CM seemed to understand what was going on with the team, but he also acknowledged that there was nothing I could do to change the circumstances. Everything had been set in motion, and I was at the point of no return. Spookily, he then told me that there was a reason behind everything happening the way they had that morning. While the reasons for those events might not yet be clear, eventually they would reveal themselves to me, he said. It was a weird conversation. I never saw him again after that meeting.

Everything happens for a reason.

Back at the team house, Horse and Eagle were downstairs in the lounge room. Bee and I went up to our room to talk through everything that had happened that morning. She had been pulled from the BIAP team, with Wolf assigned in her place.

That was when Horse appeared, looking ashen-faced. "The team has been hit," he said. "The team was stationary on Route Irish when they were hit from the side by insurgents. Camel was shot in the head and died instantly. Tomahawk was hit in the femoral artery and bled to death. Ronin is fighting for his life. It could go either way."

I ran downstairs to the team operations room to see what the vehicle configuration for the mission was and who was sitting where. There were three vehicles on the mission. Camel was driving the rear vehicle and Tomahawk was the rear gunner. Ghost was in there with them. How was it that they'd been killed, yet Ghost was okay? Ronin was in the first vehicle. What about Spitfire and Wolf, who were in there with him? What about Dr Evil and Baloo? There had been no mention of them. Were they okay?

Camel and Tomahawk were dead. Ronin could go either way.

Bee, Horse, Eagle and I gathered close together for moral support. We'd finally been hit. What the fuck had happened out there? Jeep was a mess. He couldn't think; he couldn't act. His eyes were red raw from crying and instantly I felt sorry for him; I knew he was hurting.

We went back to our rooms to await further reports. We analysed and reanalysed exactly how we thought the team must have been hit. What went on out there? Bee and I cried together. We cried for our fallen mates and we cried for Ronin, who was still fighting for his life.

I had only just told him that I had so many photos of the two of us, with me draped around his neck, that I was sure people would think we were a couple. But he was my mate. He was my friend. He was my colleague. *Hold on, Ronin.*

Camel was gone. He was only with us for a short time. He was part of the 'in crowd', just as I had been, but was beginning to see through the leaders' façade. He had already expressed his doubt about returning for another rotation, but now he was dead. His wife would be devastated. I cried for him.

I cried for Tomahawk. I walked into his room to see his sacred items lined up on his bed. He had known his fate. He'd prepared himself for death and made sure his personal effects were in order. The realisation hit me hard. Why hadn't I picked up on that when he'd said goodbye to me? I was saddened by his death, but also knew that he would move off into the afterlife with courage and pride. He had lived like a warrior and then died a warrior's death.

More news came in. Ronin was being airlifted to Camp Victory and the military medics were trying to save his life. Ghost had been hit in the arse and was also going to get treatment at Camp Victory. He had tried to save Tomahawk out on the road, but had failed. That was all we knew so far. I couldn't feel the pain of my burn. I couldn't feel anything. I was numb. We all were.

As the day progressed, more reports kept filtering back to us. Ghost was firing his MP5 around prior to the attack. A moving vehicle hit them. All sorts of snippets of information were being fed to us, but nothing could be confirmed until the team came home.

I rang Bruce at work, back in Australia. I had to tell him I was okay. I needed him to tell Kane that Mummy was not coming home today but that she was okay. I told Bruce that my team had been hit, and that due to a strange set of circumstances, I had avoided being involved in it. I couldn't tell him any details about the incident, but warned him to be prepared for the ensuing media reports.

My family thought I was going to be travelling along Route Irish that day. If they heard that an Aussie contractor from my company had been killed on the way to the airport, they would have freaked out. It was bad enough getting the 'when are you going to finish that type of work?' speech from my mum each time I spoke to her. Many contractors got that same speech from their parents each time they returned home from Iraq, but there was no answer to it. You finish when you're ready to finish. You can't put a date on it.

Jeep called us all into the lounge room. He had news. I could tell it was bad. We sat down on the chairs, then he broke it to us. Ronin had died. The medics had worked furiously on him at the hospital and he'd fought hard till the bitter end. He had lost too much blood. Bee and I hugged each other. He had been hit in the femoral artery. He held on as long as he could, but it was too much in the end.

My fallen mates. I was determined to find out what had happened. Was it bad luck or poor planning? Who had been in charge of the mission? I needed answers. We all needed answers. The families needed answers. And, by God, I was going to get them.

It was late afternoon when the team finally arrived back. It was then that Wolf showed us his videotaped version of the events, and talked us through what had happened. I sat in shocked silence as I watched the video and heard what had gone on during that trip. I sat with Wolf and watched the video over and over again. It was disturbing. As Wolf retold what happened, and had it supported by the other members of the team, I realised my worst fears had come true: leadership deficiencies had finally got my mates killed.

Ghost had been in charge of the mission. Ghost the medic was in charge of the security operation. Ghost the CAT leader was in charge of the BIAP trip. As the leader, he was responsible for the team members' lives, and ultimately their deaths.

The team had headed out late that morning for Baghdad airport. They didn't need to drop me off anymore, but they still had to pick up a client and incoming team members. The first vehicle in the team carried Wolf, Ronin and Spitfire. Wolf was assigned as the driver of the soft-skinned BMW, Ronin the vehicle commander and Spitfire the rear shooter. The next vehicle in the packet was the armoured Mercedes (or client vehicle), driven by Baloo and commanded by Dr Evil. The third vehicle was the soft-skinned BMW (or CAT vehicle). Camel was tasked as the driver, Tomahawk the rear gunner, and the medic and mission commander was Ghost.

On a good day, when traffic was flowing steadily, it could take about ten minutes to get from one end of Route Irish to the other. On a bad day, when traffic had slowed down due to army convoys on the road, it could take twenty-odd minutes to drive down. It is not a long road, but it is a dangerous one.

The team set out along Route Irish, just as they had many times before. They passed through each one of its 'RV' points, until they were stopped by the 'Big Army' (AKA the US military). An army contingent was ahead of the group and motioning for all vehicles on the road to stop in their tracks and not move any closer. This gesture was generally communicated by their pointing many machine guns in your direction. The US military was halting traffic so soldiers could investigate a suspected IED in the area. Clearance of IEDs by the military takes time. It is not a fast process. They need to ensure the safety of their own soldiers first, and then take precautions to clear the area of the IED threat. Our orders always stated that in situations such as these, the team would return to the Green Zone to wait for the road to be cleared.

As the team approached the US military on Route Irish, Ghost told them to slow down and then stop their vehicles. If you drive towards the military in any sort of unusual way, especially when you are operating in 'low profile' mode, you're likely to get shot at. Eight minutes into the trip, the team stopped the vehicles on the road. Traffic began to creep up on them, hemming them in. It was then that Ghost decided that the team was no longer going to stay low profile. He wanted to remain separate from the rest of the traffic.

He blew their cover by proceeding to fire his MP5 at the approaching traffic. An MP5 is great for using in buildings and other confined spaces because of the range and velocity of the weapon. In open environments, such as out on Route Irish, the M-4 rifle, the Austeyr and even an AK-47 are far better weapons to use. They can fire out to greater distances; they have a greater impact on the target area and are far more accurate. The MP5 is designed to accurately fire out to 25 metres; at best it could effectively hit a target at 50 metres. You'd be hard pressed to hit anything at 100, let alone 200 metres.

Impractical or otherwise, that MP5 held a special place in Ghost's heart. It was short barrelled so it was easier for him to handle in the vehicle. He didn't have to worry about an M-4, with its long, cumbersome barrel. He had pimped his MP5 with a rail system, optical sight and all sorts of attachments. It was useless on Route Irish, but it looked cool.

Ghost used his MP5 to warn off nearby vehicles. All traffic halted immediately. Nine and a half minutes into the trip, and all three cars had become identifiable as part of a Western security team. Now all the team members were sitting ducks. They were left vulnerable and exposed as they sat on the road, waiting for the IED to be cleared. And there they continued to sit. As time went by, cars again began to creep closer to them. Ghost fired more warning shots.

Tick-tock, another sixteen minutes went by. A white sedan from in front of the team started to cross the median strip to turn around and go back the other way. Three more minutes went by. It was at this stage that Ghost considered driving over the median strip to go around the Big Army. He considered it, but did nothing. Instead, two minutes later, Ghost got out of his vehicle to fire more shots at another nearby car. What he didn't realise was that his 'commander phone' had fallen out of his pocket, landing on the ground. After dealing with the Iraqi driver, he got back into his vehicle to await route clearance.

Then more vehicles from in front of the team started turning around and crossing the median strip. With the vehicles in front leaving the area, the team inched their vehicles forwards. They didn't get very far before they came to a sudden stop, as they had moved too close to the US military. There they sat: a total of twenty-five minutes remaining stationary on one of the world's most dangerous roads.

It was at this point that Ghost noticed that he'd lost his mobile phone. Slowly the realisation set in that it must have fallen out when he fired his warning shots at the other cars. After thinking about his predicament for a moment, he decided they should turn around and go back for it. He was too late. They had been exposed out on the road for too long. A loud *crack* whipped through the air and thundered deep into their car.

Immediately, the vehicle was bombarded with bullets. Camel was shot in the thigh and head, and died instantly. Tomahawk returned fire with his weapon, but was ineffective due to being mortally wounded in the initial volley of enemy fire. He valiantly tried to evacuate the vehicle under fire, but he didn't stand a chance. The enemy bullets penetrated the soft-skinned vehicle like hungry coyotes rushing in for the kill. Tomahawk slumped in his seat, and was slowly bleeding to death.

Ghost took a round to his arse, grabbed his MP5 and started firing it in the direction of the insurgents. Luckily, he managed to avoid being fatally shot. He jumped out of his vehicle, and ran around to check on Camel. He was dead. Tomahawk was still breathing, so Ghost grabbed his medical kit and began to work on him.

At the same time, the advance vehicle was also being hit. The enemy bullets sliced through the soft-skinned vehicle. Ronin was hit. Spitfire and Ronin returned fire, aiming their rounds in the direction of the 'suspect vehicle'. Wolf tried to start the car, but it wouldn't move. Being a manual vehicle, it had been placed in neutral gear while it became stationary. Wolf had ridden the clutch for the first fifteen minutes of waiting, but his leg cramped up after such a considerable time. He placed it into neutral, expecting to remain stationary for at least another hour, as they had during previous operations under Ghost's leadership.

After realising the vehicle was possibly disabled, the advance team reverted back to their actions on 'disabled vehicle'. They needed to get out and withdraw to a safe position. Being the closest to the 'safe' side of the vehicle, Wolf exited first, while Ronin and Spitfire continued to return fire. When in position, Wolf returned fire, and the other two also began to exit the vehicle. Ronin fired all his rounds, reloaded, and then fired again. He struggled heroically to pull his injured body from out of the car. He then took up a fire position and kept shooting until he eventually passed out.

When Spitfire exited the vehicle, Wolf withdrew to another fire position, and returned fire. He called for Spitfire to follow, but the enemy fire had died down. Meanwhile, Baloo and Dr Evil had been returning fire and attempting to move their vehicle forwards to provide additional cover to the advance team. The armoured vehicle was hit several times, with rounds almost penetrating Dr Evil's door. The car eventually moved forwards, and they rushed out to assist the team. Spitfire tended to Ronin, his best mate, and furiously tried to save his life.

It was a futile effort. It was too late. The damage had been done. Tomahawk, Camel and Ronin passed away on 20 April 2005.

My mates were gone and there was nothing I could do. The moment was unreal to me. Do you know how sometimes you just wait for the time when you can say, "I told you so?" Well, that time had arrived, and I couldn't do it. I was sick with rage and resentment, but I couldn't say it. I didn't have to say it. Everyone already knew it.

When the team returned later that day, we were all told that nobody was at fault. We were told that no one was to blame, except for the insurgents. They were right. The insurgents killed my friends. They were men with no honour, no respect and no value for life. They killed because they wanted to. It didn't matter if their victims were Western or Arabs. They killed their own people as often as they did foreigners. For what? They didn't fight for freedom, honour, equality and everything else I have come to enjoy in my life. Instead, they fought for power, money and control.

Insurgents were to blame for the deaths of my mates, but the team's safety was the responsibility of my leaders and my company. That failure has left me bitter and angry to this day. Poor planning, poor leadership, poor tactics, poor judgment and poor capabilities were in evidence throughout my time on the team. As a security team, we were supposed to avoid risk, and run our operations as safely as possible. It was blatantly obvious this was not happening, and finally it led to the deaths of my colleagues. Conducting unnecessarily risky operations didn't make you 'tough'. It made you stupid.

Poor Baloo admitted to me that his car was in neutral, and that was why he couldn't move the armoured vehicle in the initial volley of fire. I told him it wasn't his fault. Team vehicle training would have addressed that problem. Luckily, he was in an automatic transmission car, so he was able to remedy the problem quickly despite his vehicle also suffering from 'catastrophic' engine failure. Trained close protection operatives are taught that automatic transmission cars are the best vehicles to use on missions because if you are attacked, the stress and surprise of the incident is generally going to make you stall your car. Additionally, when stationary, you are taught to leave the vehicle in gear and keep your foot on the brake. That way, when you are attacked, your instinct will be to step on the accelerator and get yourself out of the line of fire. Baloo got lucky, but Wolf didn't have a hope in hell. Even if his handbrake had not been on when they were hit, I'm sure he would have stalled the manual transmission car, and still ended up in the same position.

The company put on a final hurrah for Tomahawk, Camel and Ronin that night. They supplied alcohol and food. It was held at the team house, under the Christmas fairy lights. And then I drank. I drank, and I cried, and I hugged my teammates. Before I knew it, Horse was holding my head out of bucket as I spewed. I cried each time I vomited into the bucket. I was angry with all the leaders, and how they had contributed to what had happened that day. I was also angry at myself for not being able to do a dammed thing about it.

My instincts about the team leaders had served me well. Thank God I had refused Red Zone missions with my team. Thank God I had awkwardly spilt boiling water down the front of me that morning. If I hadn't been so clumsy, I would have been on that mission. I could have been killed. Even worse, I could have been stuck in the middle of the firefight, without a weapon, watching my mates die. I vowed never to forget what those leaders had done.

I couldn't wait to leave the country. A few days later I caught a lift back with another team. They gave me body armour, a helmet, webbing and a rifle. I got onto the aircraft and slept all the way back home.

When I saw Kane, I hugged him with all my might. I needed my little boy to help bring me back to the real world. He was my sanity and my reality check. I pushed the pain of what had happened way back into the recesses of my mind, and focused completely on him. It was time to be a mum and let the warrior woman sleep.

The next few months in Australia were a welcome relief. Bruce and Pamela were still insisting that I live with them, and I was happy to take them up on the offer. We were building a really solid friendship between the three of us. Each morning I would drop off Kane and his stepsister Sonya at school. I'd then go for a run, have a shower and change. By the time I had finished, Pamela would be up with her new baby girl, Sapphire (Kane's half-sister), and then we'd have a coffee together. It was the simple life.

Not sure if I wanted to return to Iraq to work again, I left for South Africa to complete the Ronin close protection course. It was everything I'd hoped it would be and more. The medical and weapons components of the course were top quality. Due to all the safety protocols in the military sometimes training can be restrictive. But in South Africa, I did things I would not normally have been able to. I fired left-handed, right-handed, in daylight, and in darkness. I shot from moving vehicles, I shot while running from cover to cover, and I shot while protecting my client. It was undoubtedly the best weapons course I'd ever done.

By the time I left, I had learnt new methods for providing protection and gained some valuable medical and weaponry skills. I felt confident that I could get a job anywhere in the world. How many women can say they have completed the elite MP close protection course, as well as the Ronin course? Bugger that, how many men can say the same?

I returned to Australia, and a spent another few months staying with Bruce and Pamela. My feet were getting itchy, though. I had enough money to buy a small unit in Cairns (to store my furniture in), but not quite enough for a decent-sized house in Canberra. I had to go back to work. I contacted Lizard and arrangements were made to go and work for Blackwater. He'd moved on to other work by that stage, but he made his incumbent country manager aware of who I was, and what my skills were.

On 11 September 2005, I left Australia. I was concerned about what awaited me back in Iraq. Would my old team still be there? Would I work in the same area? What would I do if I saw Jeep, Ghost or Merlin again?

Blackwater was more organised by far than my old company. It was also larger and had better capabilities, such as its own aircraft and pilots. No more having to stuff around at airports and fight to get onto planes. Blackwater was flying me and other contractors into Baghdad. In Jordan, we were walked step-by-step through all the airport procedures, and then shown aboard. I felt safe and secure among my colleagues, and knew that my company was taking good care of me.

We flew into Baghdad airport and were greeted by the team responsible for transporting us to the Green Zone. They had huge armoured vehicles, with guns mounted on top for all-round protection. The team was friendly, if a little taken aback at the sight of me. They were surprised that the company had hired a woman, but agreed it was a good idea, considering many of their clients were female.

After being issued with some equipment, I received a quick set of orders, and then we set out to the Green Zone. There was none of this shit about "driving as fast as you could to get the other side". I was given arcs of responsibility to cover with my weapon, and I was informed of what to do if the vehicle was disabled. I knew where the medical kit was, where the spare ammo was, and what was expected of me.

We arrived at the Green Zone without incident. I gathered my equipment (which was not much, as my luggage hadn't made it to Jordan) and went in to speak with the new country manager, Judas. Judas was a tall, well-built American. He had a goatee (as did most of the Americans I met), and warm eyes. He welcomed me into the company and handed me a 'contractors' code of conduct' pamphlet. It listed guidelines that all employees were to follow while working for the company. I was impressed, to say the least. Here I was, in the middle of a war zone, working for a company that had taken active steps to be responsible and accountable. What a far cry that was from my previous job!

Judas promised me that he'd make enquiries on my behalf about my missing luggage, but, in the meantime, I'd have to make do with what I had. I was hastily introduced to my team, before being squashed into the back of an armoured car and transported out to the Red Zone. Our team house was located in the Karrada district, not far from the entrance to the Green Zone. The site had its own security, which comprised both local and Western security guards. It was also heavily fortified with massive firepower capabilities. I was introduced to the rest of team, my gender surprising pretty much everyone there. But I was used to it: it was just another day in the life of a minority.

I was shown to my room, which was located in a house separate from the main headquarters. The compound I worked in was composed of several houses, all located on the one street. Our section of the district was blocked off by several security points so it was relatively safe to walk from house to house. Nevertheless body armour was always used, especially when escorting clients around the area. I was shown to my room and introduced to the guy I would be sharing with.

Scooter was a tall American, with blond hair and blue eyes. He was married, a Mormon, and had a deep Southern drawl. I was paired up with him as he was voted the 'least likely to put the moves on me'. I listened to this with a smirk on my face. It was such a male thing to think! I wasn't interested in any kind of attention from men. If I were ever going to have a man in my life, he'd have to be a Canberran. There was no way Bruce would ever agree to my moving somewhere else with Kane, especially with his taking responsibility for him while I was away.

No, I was here to do my job and make some money. I just needed enough for a decent-sized deposit (and then a little extra), so I could retire from the business and get a 'real job'. I'd probably only need to do this rotation plus one more before I could hang up my gun for good.

I settled into my room, using one of my cupboards as a divider between our bed spaces. I had a couple of trunks that I'd left with Bee, which contained personal weapons, clothes and other equipment. Thank goodness I had a few pairs of pants in there. I'd been wearing the same ones for the past three days. With my luggage still missing, I could not change clothes. I was beginning to smell so I went to take a quick shower.

Feeling refreshed, I unpacked the rest of my equipment and settled into my room. There was a huge TV in our room, with two armchairs facing towards it. *Man, were we going to be comfortable.* I sat down and chatted to Scooter, and slowly we got to know each other better. The same old questions came out. *What's your training? Who have you worked for? How long have been in country? Are you married? Do you have children?*

Scooter was an ex–US MP member. We had that in common. He had served over here with the military, but was now content to work as a contractor: the money was better, as were the working conditions. That was about it. He wanted what we all did – enough money to set himself up. He wanted to own his own home and then he could just 'survive' on normal wages. It was the mantra of every contractor: do the hard yards now, and then enjoy life mortgage-free.

I asked Scooter about the job, and he talked me through it. While here, we would escort clients around the area (they worked from another building located in the compound). At times we'd have to send a full team into the Green Zone with the clients so they could attend meetings. Sometimes we'd have to make BIAP trips to pick up and drop off clients at the airport, or maybe to get supplies from the PX store.

Our team employed low-profile drills, meaning we drove and mixed with the local traffic. Being tasked as a driver on my team, I soon learnt how things went on the Red Zone roads. I'd weave in and out of traffic, cut cars off, drive at ridiculous speeds, hog the road, and generally do everything I wouldn't dare to in Australia. It was crazy, but necessary, and everybody did it. It was how things worked in Iraq.

I was going to enjoy working on this contract. I liked my teammates, I liked my job and I liked my company. Thank God not all teams operated like my last. If this one had been the same, I would have quit on the spot. There was no way I'd put myself through that kind of crap again. This team was operating like a team. The leaders were competent; they gave good orders and intelligence briefings, and cared about each member. I knew I was in safe hands.

The next three weeks cruised by at an amazing rate. The team was being supplied with new armoured vehicles, worth hundreds of thousands of dollars each. We were tasked to drive out to the BIAP to pick them up. Our project had three separate teams, each one allocated different tasks and missions moving clients around. All three teams would be required for this task. As the vehicles were brand-new, shiny and black – far too recognisable as Western vehicles – the low-profile approach was tossed out the window.

It was decided we'd complete this mission in high-profile fashion. We were to be heavily armed and visibly aggressive. No vehicles would be permitted to enter our 'safety bubble'. Warning shots were to be fired in front of offending vehicles, taking care not to injure anyone. If a driver refused to back away, we would fire at the engine blocks to disable the vehicle. The lethal option was to be employed as a last resort – only to be used if we felt our lives were in danger.

If a local Iraqi driver refused to back off after shots had been fired firstly in front of their vehicle, and then secondly at their engine block, it was a safe bet that they were dangerous – they were most likely to be a suicide bomber or the catalyst for an attack. Either way, no innocent person would continue driving towards a convoy that was firing shots in their direction.

On this particular trip, I was located in the rear vehicle of the convoy, operating as a rear shooter with another guy. We took several slip roads in the Red Zone, before finding ourselves stuck at a set of traffic lights. We were dislocated from the rest of the convoy, and couldn't proceed further due to traffic blockages in front of us. How we ended up like that, I have no idea. I was too busy looking out the rear of the vehicle to know. We were edgy. Our driver was looking for a break in traffic so he could push his way through to the rest of the team.

I was in the back, looking behind me, when I spotted a vehicle full of armed, hooded locals. Straightaway I alerted the vehicle commander: a white Nissan Patrol was approaching us. The rear tray contained about five locals, armed with AK-47s, and all wearing balaclavas. *This is it*, I thought to myself. If these dodgy bastards weren't insurgents, I don't know who were. They inched towards us, and shots were fired. The guy sitting next to me let off a few warning shots, and immediately the Nissan slowed down.

Other vehicles around us made an effort to drive away from us. As it was an armoured vehicle, the rear windows did not roll down. So I cracked my door open slightly, ready to light up the insurgents if they returned fire. I was shitting myself. I didn't want to kill someone if I didn't have to, but if they pointed their weapons in my direction, I would let them have it.

Fortunately, it didn't come to that. The lights changed colour, and we sped off to catch up to the rest of the team. The insurgents never caught up to us; perhaps they had another mission they had to complete. It was thought that they might have been Iraqi police, as they had recently commenced patrolling Route Irish. They often wore balaclavas to hide their identities from insurgents, and protect themselves and their families. These guys didn't wear uniforms and their vehicle wasn't labelled as police either. In the end, we didn't know, but we were not going to take any chances.

We got to the BIAP and picked up all five shiny, new black armoured cars. They were awesome. They were pure luxury inside and had incredible power under the hood. On return to the base, they would be painted a dull off-white so they would blend in with traffic a little easier. They wouldn't be as inconspicuous as a beat-up old BMW, but their profile would be lowered.

We were all assigned vehicles to drive (or be a passenger in) for the return trip. There were only just enough people to do the job. Each vehicle had a driver and a passenger. I was located in the rear vehicle with the team leader, Church. He was the driver, and I was his rear security for both our vehicle and our team. My job was to shoot at any vehicle that got too close.

We started back to base with little drama. Shortly after leaving, however, we received a distress message from the vehicle in front of us. The car was an old armoured BMW and the driver was having problems with the engine. It was losing power and couldn't continue at a high speed. The driver went on to say that he thought he could keep pushing it until we got to the Green Zone, but that he couldn't go faster than 30 kilometres an hour.

The convoy slowed to a crawl and very quickly traffic banked up behind us. We started to drive in a zigzag fashion across the road so as not to make ourselves easy targets for insurgents. A large truck began to creep up towards our vehicle. Was his truck laden with explosives? I cracked open my door and aimed my M-4 rifle at the driver's head. I then lowered it and fired a round into the road in front of him. Instantly, he put his hands up in the air and backed the truck away. No more cars crept up on us after that.

Some days were tense, and some days were easy. We were paid the same no matter what. It had been a tense trip that day, but for the next week I managed to fit in watching an entire season of *Alias* with Scooter. We made another hairy trip out to the airport while I was there, but this time there were no bad guys involved.

Our team was tasked to pick up a client from the airport. We were part way along Route Irish when we got a flat tyre. Not willing to stop on the road and risk death, we had no choice but to continue on. We kept driving, but at a slower speed, until the rubber fell off the wheel. We didn't know how long we could keep going before we'd need to change the tyre. Worse still, the traffic we'd zoomed past was now catching up to us. The driver, 86, then had a brainwave. He began to drive partly on the road and partly on the dirt. The dirt kicked up a huge dust storm behind us, creating just the smokescreen we needed.

It was an excellent way to discourage other vehicles from approaching us too closely from behind. No one wanted to risk driving through a dust storm to find out what was on the other side. Sparks flew from the damaged wheel, and the dirt billowed behind us. It would have been an awesome sight from afar.

We managed to make it to the checkpoint at Camp Victory, where we pulled off to the side of the road to change the tyre. As we worked furiously to do it quickly, several PSD teams passed us by. Some made jokes, some offered assistance and others just stared and drove past. For weeks after the incident, there were a hell of a lot of PSD guys asking me if I was the chick changing the tyre on Route Irish. I guess I still wasn't as nondescript as I had hoped.

It was hard to just be a normal chick in such a testosterone-charged environment like Iraq. I liked being with my team, and when we went out together, no one would 'bother' me or try to chat me up because I had my mates there to rebuff them. When I was alone, though, I was like carrion to a bunch of vultures. Everyone wanted to make small talk with me. I didn't blame them or anything. It's hard working in a place where there aren't many people of the opposite sex.

Whether they were military personnel or civilian contractors, it didn't matter, I was practically having to beat them away with a stick. I was getting embarrassed by the attention. It wasn't that I was amazingly beautiful or anything like that, I was just female. There was nothing I could do about it, except leave, of course, and I wasn't prepared to do that just yet. Until then, I would have to deal with the marriage proposals from soldiers at checkpoints, and the endless chitchat with complete strangers.

Being part of a team that worked well together was a great feeling. Knowing that I could trust my leadership and my teammates was still a novelty, and I didn't take it for granted. Each mission we completed, we did well. We went to the University of Baghdad and protected our clients as they gave lectures. We took them to hotels within the Red Zone, and protected them there. There were near misses, such as the time a client cancelled his lecture at a local hotel. Two hours later it was destroyed by a car bomb. Lucky client. Lucky team.

Not every mission I did with the team was 'sanctioned' by the company. I'd be lying if I said we never conducted 'black ops' or rogue operations that ran contrary to our duty statement. While we never did anything iniquitous, we did go on one or two unauthorised operations.

Operation Ice-Cream was one of our most desperate missions. It was 9.15 p.m. We were sitting in the common room of our house, with the clients fast asleep, or at least done for the day. We were having a bit of a team get-together, which involved teasing each other, chatting about other teams and talking about home. Out of the blue, the subject of ice-cream came up. I remarked on how I could really do with an ice-cream just then, and one of the team leaders piped up that there was an ice-cream shop down the road.

Now 'down the road' meant outside of our safe compound, onto the main road, and down a bit further than that. One minute we were talking about ice-cream, and then the next, we were planning an ad hoc mission. I won't mention any of the names associated with this rogue outfit – after all, it was black ops – but we filled two cars. We got dressed in all our kit, and headed out into the night.

The road was mainly empty. Only a few cars were travelling this late at night, but people were still roaming the streets. As we approached the ice-cream store, we noticed several patrons were wandering around outside. It was the place to be at night! We pulled up right in front of the shop and exited our vehicles, just as we'd planned.

The drivers remained in the vehicles, with the engines on and the cars in gear, while the rest of us got into diamond formation around the guy doing the ordering. I remained close to him, as his bodyguard, as he proceeded to order banana, strawberry and chocolate waffles. The local people standing around were shocked and amused by what they saw. A team of big, tough Western security contractors, out and about after dark, ordering ice-cream.

An Iraqi policeman was sitting down on a nearby bench, watching with glee. After the orders had been placed and paid for, we left immediately. We tear-arsed our way back home, and found ourselves sitting in the common room eating ice-cream within fifteen minutes of leaving.

While the identities of my black ops team will always remain a secret, I will confirm that the ice-cream was absolutely delicious. The honeycomb waffles, covered in rich chocolate ice-cream, were to *die for*. Hey, what's wrong with a little black humour? Okay, it wouldn't have been so funny if I had actually been killed getting it, but surely it's a little bit funny now? No?

My life on the team was going great. I was considered a valuable and good team member. That was all I'd ever wanted. I just wanted to be accepted for my skills. I was no one special, but I was competent enough to do my job well. I was fitting in and my teammates were accepting of me. Life was good. I could last another rotation if these were my working conditions. I didn't have to deal with any of the crap I experienced with my last team. These guys were professional.

But all good things come to an end. Just when I thought my life was back on track, it was as if fate noticed and wanted to bring me down a peg or two. It started the day my company decided to move me to a more 'female-friendly' environment. Not long after that my worst nightmare came true.

After a month of my working with my team, it was decided I should be moved into the Green Zone. We had clients living there who also required protection. I would be responsible for coordinating their moves and ensuring their security at certain venues. The project manager, K2, believed it would be the best option for me as they would be able to provide me with my own trailer. I would no longer be required to share a room or bathroom facilities.

I was disappointed. I would miss working with the rest of the team. I would still see them when they came into the Green Zone for missions, but it wouldn't be the same. I would now be working more as a bodyguard/personal assistant than as a team member. It would be great having my own room, but I would miss the friends I'd made.

I packed up all my kit and said goodbye to my teammates. They proceeded to tell me about the other two guys from their project who were already in the Green Zone working with the clients. The first man was named Spoon. He had arrived on the team telling everyone he wanted to be called 'Blade' (because he loved knives and had a huge collection). Being so full of himself, Church promptly gave him the call sign 'Spoon' instead.

The other man on the team was named Wingnut. They didn't like him at all. He had only worked on their team for a short period of time, but he did not fit in. They sent him over to the Green Zone to work in the same position as mine so they wouldn't have to deal with him. I asked them what was wrong with him, and the response was that he was a loser. I kept their observations in the back of my mind, as I always like to come to my own conclusions about a person.

My team drove me over to the Green Zone and dropped me off in a heavily fortified compound. I grabbed my kit, said my goodbyes and introduced myself to the two other guys. Spoon was in charge at the time, and he showed me to my trailer. He was a tall, friendly Native American. His claim to fame was that he'd had a bit part in the 1994 *Stargate* movie with Kurt Russell and James Spader. Spoon made sure I had everything I needed, and then took me on a tour of the compound. He explained that we shared the compound with another company named Unity Resources Group (URG), but that they lived in a separate section to us.

He told me our job was mainly concerned with transporting our clients around the Green Zone. Sometimes we would be required to escort them to certain places, but, for the most part, we were able to just drop them off at a secure building for their meetings. It was a pretty good job with lots of spare time, he said. We had to be on-call all the time, but when we weren't driving the clients around, our time was our own. It sounded like a good gig to me.

A few hours later, I was introduced to Wingnut. He was short, stocky and had hair protruding from his shirt collar. He smoked like a chimney, drank coffee like it was water and sweated profusely. Once he started talking, he didn't stop. He seemed friendly enough and proceeded to fill me in on all the gossip about the clients, the company and its new projects. I mentioned that I was into running so he organised for us to go to the gym in the mornings before work.

I would finally get some regular exercise in each day, and have a fairly easy job of escorting clients around the area. It was certainly not as dangerous as driving around the Red Zone or doing BIAP trips. Things were looking up. Wingnut asked me to accompany him on several security trips that day so that he could introduce me to the clients.

The first client I was met was Jar Jar, a tall, blond, athletic American. He loved to talk too, and was extremely friendly and courteous. He understood the security constraints he was bound by, and did his best to inform us of his daily itinerary. The other client, Olive, was a mess. She was scatterbrained, oblivious to the security situation and condescending towards all the security staff. She was the main reason I had been brought onto the project.

The next two days passed relatively quickly. I drove my clients around to various venues, and began settling into my new way of life. On day three of my new job, Wingnut and I went to the gym for a work-out. He was really perky. I asked him why he was so jolly, and he replied that he was just feeling good from all the gym work. I shrugged, thinking he was overdosing on endorphins, and went and trashed myself on the treadmill for thirty minutes. After a short weights session, we returned to our compound.

We were walking back to our trailers just as Spoon was getting up. He was on the lookout for coffee, and Wingnut had the freshest, hottest stuff available. So my gym buddy went to his room to turn on the coffee percolator, while I had a quick shower. A short time later, Spoon and I knocked on his door, with our coffee cups in hand. We needed caffeine. Wingnut answered the door with the steaming coffee pot in hand. He poured us our coffees, and we sat down to chat.

Wingnut lit up a cigarette and started sucking down the tar. Spoon told me that there was a barbecue on later that night and that we were required to attend. The barbecue was just around the corner from our trailers, so at least we didn't have to travel too far. We would be allowed to have a couple of drinks that night, and I thought it might be good to meet some of the other security people working in the area. I thought back to the advice about networking Spitfire had given me, what seemed like a lifetime ago: you never knew when you might need to change jobs.

Wingnut was still really full of beans. He continued to sweat buckets, even as we sat on the stairs of our trailers. I had never seen anything like it. As soon as he'd wipe his brow, more beads of sweat would magically appear on his forehead. It didn't take long for his shirt to soak through, but he didn't seem too concerned. I asked him again why he was so happy. He was talkative, bouncy and just seemed so pleased with himself. He said it was the endorphins from working out, but did allude to having found the right combination of 'uppers'. I didn't really know what he meant by that, but the last thing I wanted was to find out that another team member was taking drugs. I left him to himself and went to look after my clients.

I finished working late in the afternoon. I rang up Bee and told her to come around to my trailer. She lived a short distance away from where I was staying, and knew my compound well. There was a restaurant located there, and it was quite popular.

The food wasn't that good, but it was a place people could go to have a few drinks together.

Bee came over about 7.30 p.m. I introduced her to Spoon, and then took her into my room. I took off my pistol and ammunition and placed them on my cupboard. I poured some drinks for Bee and me, and then gave the gifts I'd brought her from home. I gave her an 'Australia' hat, a sloppy joe, a bracelet and a mood ring. We chatted about everything we'd been up to since I'd left the country, and gossiped about our old team. The company had ended up losing their contract, and so all the guys were sent home. It was a relief to know that there was no chance I'd be bumping into Jeep, Ghost or any of the other leaders.

Some of the 'good' team members had gone on to other jobs, and I'd even run into a few of them. Mr Happy was on a new contract, as was Spitfire and Horse. I didn't know what had happened to everyone else, but I doubted I'd see their faces again. As we were chatting, Wingnut came into my room and made himself a drink. I had plenty of ice in my freezer and was the only person who had any Coke to mix with the drinks. I introduced the two, and then Wingnut left.

Bee hung around for a while before she also had to go, but we made plans to catch up later on in the week. The barbecue had still not been cooked so I poured myself another drink. I sat out on the stairs of my trailer and joined in the conversation with Spoon and Wingnut. We sat there for the next forty minutes, chatting about our jobs, about security matters, and how different it was having a woman on the team. It was a conversation I enjoyed, as it gave me the opportunity to enlighten them about all the things a woman could offer the team.

I must have dribbled on for quite some time, because at 9 p.m. we were called over to get some food. I poured myself one last drink before heading over. With my drink in hand, I walked to the barbecue with Spoon and Wingnut. I was introduced to quite a few people before I was finally able to grab myself a steak sandwich. Skippy was in charge of the barbecue. He was our contact for all issues concerning our trailers. He was the team leader of the other security team, but he was also responsible for the accommodation we were renting.

Skippy had white-blond hair, a terrific sense of humour and, most importantly, he was Aussie. It was great to chat to someone from home, as most of the guys I worked with were Americans. It was good to be able to talk to someone who wasn't constantly asking me to 'translate' what I was saying. You'd be surprised at how often I would have to explain myself to my American buddies. Often my old teammate Scooter would say to me, "I see your lips moving, and I can hear your voice talking, but I have no idea what you are saying."

I chatted to a few other people that night, including Jar Jar and a woman named April. She was very curious about women working in the security field and, in particular, this environment. She was a client on Skippy's contract and was fascinated by the whole thing. By 10 p.m. we were ready to leave.

Wingnut, Spoon and I returned to our trailers and sat on the stairs, continuing our conversation. I'd had three drinks by now and was feeling quite chatty. It was at this point that I made the worst mistake of my life. Over the past few days I had grown to trust my new teammates. In this job, trusting your teammate was essential to being able to perform your job. If you couldn't trust the person you worked with, how could you work together to fight the enemy?

Well, I made the mistake of trusting my teammate enough to allow him to pour me another drink. Wingnut went into his room to get another cup, or so I thought, and then into my room to make another drink. He returned a short time later and handed it to me. I had no reason to think he was up to no good. I had no reason not to trust him. But after my first sip of that drink, things suddenly became hazy.

I took a sip from the drink Wingnut handed me, and then my life changed forever. I remember Spoon saying goodnight and going to bed at some point. I know I sat on the stairs for quite some time, talking, gossiping and calling Wingnut "my mate". He handed me another drink. I swallowed one mouthful and that was enough. I told Wingnut I was feeling sick, and that I was going to bed. Four drinks that night were ample for me. I got up and walked into my trailer. I closed the door and went to the bathroom.

The next thing I knew, I was vomiting in the toilet. I couldn't understand why I was so sick. I hadn't drunk that much. Wingnut must have come into my room because I heard him call out to me through the door.

"Are you okay?" he asked.

"I'm fine," I told him. "I'm just a little sick." By the time I came out of the bathroom, Wingnut had left my room.

Feeling totally out of it, I collapsed on my bed. Passing out was the last thing I remembered, before waking up in pain. It was dark. Something was hurting me deep inside. *Oh my God. There is someone in my bed with me.* My mind was muddled. I could feel a deep scratching along the left-hand side of my insides. Something was penetrating me. It was hurting. I winced in pain and moved my body. I couldn't see anything. It was dark, my mind was fuzzy and I was fighting hard to stay conscious.

Suddenly the pain stopped and I blacked out again. The dark netherworld took hold and delivered me into sweet oblivion. But it was not for long. I awoke at some later stage, and this time I could see a dark figure on top of me. I froze. I tried not to breathe. I didn't who it was. The figure put his hand under my shirt and pulled up my bra. His face, his hands, they were all over me. He crept higher up me until his chest was covering me, smothering me, overpowering me. I turned my head, afraid he'd kiss my face, afraid of the closeness, and incapable of getting away.

His arms were suffocating me; his foul stench was invading my senses. I began to cry as I realised what was happening. The dark figure pulled my underwear to the side, and then he raped me. I couldn't do anything. I was frozen. I couldn't move. *Why can't I move? Does he have a gun? Where is mine? Who is this person?* I tried to stay awake. I had to focus on who this person was. The black oblivion was calling me; it was pulling me into the world of sleep. I had to fight the urge to black out. I had to fight.

He stopped. He must have noticed my tears and quiet sniffling. He rose up onto his elbows and looked down at me. It was then I realised who he was. Small rays of moonlight filtered through the window, and I could see that the person was Wingnut. Wingnut was on top of me. He was infecting me: his hairy chest, his sweaty body, his foul, cigarette-smelling breath. He was hurting me. He was raping me. He was stripping away my dignity. I blacked out again: the sweet escape from reality.

I felt the bed moving. I opened my eyes. The light was on and Wingnut was getting off my bed.

"Don't tell anyone what happened," I heard him say. Then he left my room.

I grabbed my phone and got back under the covers. I tried to ring someone. Anyone. The phone wasn't working. Each time I dialled a number, the phone would send a message saying that the network was down. *Fuck Iraq and its unreliable communications system.*

As I was dialling, Wingnut re-entered my room: "Are you trying to ring someone?"

"No! Go away!" I yelled. I could feel my bed move. I panicked and jumped off my bed and raced straight into my bathroom. I slammed the door shut and quickly locked it behind me. *Fuck!* My gun was back in my room somewhere. *Fuck!* Did he have his gun? I crouched down in the shower recess, in case he decided to shoot me through the wall.

I tapped away at my phone. *Why the fuck wasn't it working?* My mind was still jumbled. I was crying and cursing, as I hurriedly tried to ring somebody. It seemed like an eternity before I finally got through to 86. God knows how long I sat, curled up on the floor of my shower, trying to ring someone.

"Thank God I got you, 86." He was a member of my Red Zone team. "I need help," I stuttered. "I've been raped." I broke down and cried; 86 tried to get as much information as possible from me, but it was difficult due to my emotional state.

"Who did it?" he asked.

"It was Wingnut," I told him.

I told him I was locked in my bathroom and too afraid to leave. My gun was out on the cupboard and I didn't know if he was outside, waiting to shoot me. I still wasn't thinking clearly. My mind was still scrambled. I was a mess. I cried into the phone and didn't stop until I heard a knock at my door.

"There's someone at my door," I told 86.

"It should be K2 and Judas. We've contacted them and told them to get to you straightaway."

"Who is it?" I called out through the door.

"It's K2," I heard the voice say.

Slowly, I unlocked the door and opened it a crack. It was indeed K2 and Judas, my senior contract staff. I then realised I had no pants on. I needed some clothes.

"Can you get me my pants?" I asked.

K2 grabbed my crushed cargos and passed them to me. I put them on, and then gradually came out of the bathroom. I was embarrassed to be seen. I was ashamed and humiliated.

"I didn't say no," I told them. "I just let it happen. I didn't want it to happen, but I didn't say no. I did nothing. I just froze up. My head's not right. I want to go back to my old room. The one I shared with Scooter. I want to lie in my bed and go to sleep. I want to go back to my team. I'm safe with them. Let me go back to Scooter's room. My team will make sure no one ever hurts me again," I begged.

I was disgusted with myself. Why did I freeze up? I prided myself on being tough and stronger than the average woman. Why didn't I fight back? Why did I just let it happen? My mind was still fuzzy. I had trusted Wingnut. He was my teammate. How could he do this? I was in one hell of an emotional state. K2 called Bee, and she accompanied me to the US medical facility. We were taken into a room, where I was examined. I was questioned by K2 and Judas. I was questioned by the military police. I was questioned by the nurse. I was questioned by Bee. Everyone wanted and needed to know what had happened.

My urine was tested for your run-of-the-mill drugs, but nothing out of the ordinary was detected. For some reason, no one took a blood test. I would have thought it was necessary to check my blood alcohol level and to test for any other 'exotic' drugs. I knew by that stage Wingnut had put something in my drink. There was no other explanation. I poured myself three drinks in two and a half hours. They were all normal nips and should not have affected me much. Whatever he put in my drink after those first three, wiped me out completely.

Wingnut had poured my drinks after my initial three. Either he slipped something into them, or he filled them mostly with alcohol and the tiniest bit of Coke. Whichever it was, it made me violently sick and unable to fight back. He had been so high since that morning. It was as if he had decided on a plan of action and was happy with what he had decided. It was all beginning to make sense now.

The dirty little troll had planned to rape me. There was no way in hell I was going to let him get away with it. He might have robbed me of my will when he drugged and then raped me, but there was no way he was going to stop me from lodging a police report. I'd make sure he'd go to jail for his crime.

He was a disgusting, pitiful creature who preyed on unsuspecting people. He needed to be stopped. God knows how many women he'd done it to before; and God knows how many more he was going to do it to again. I didn't care how humiliated and violated I would feel throughout the court process, I was not going to let him intimidate me and get away with it.

I left the hospital in a borrowed PT kit. My shirt, pants, underwear and socks were taken away for evidence. I emerged from the examination room in a pair of shorts and a shirt. K2 organised for me to stay with Bee for a few days until the company could sort things out. Bee was now working as a high-level security director so she had a lot of power within the industry. She took me to her compound and gave me a room. I showered, scrubbing myself until I got the foul stench of cigarette smoke off my body. I scrubbed to rid myself of his touch, his thoughts, his everything. I collapsed in my bed and slept fitfully for the next few hours.

I awoke with a start. It took me a little time to work out where I was and what was going on. As soon as I remembered what had happened, I curled up in ball and cried. I felt so drained. I couldn't let what had happened affect me. I knew I'd been through far worse. My break-up with Bruce had cut me up emotionally. Working for my previous cowboy team had cut me up. There was no way I was going to let this rape cut me up too.

He may have taken me physically, but there was no way he was going to get through to my mind and my soul. A barrier had gone up years ago, and there was no way I was going to let him penetrate that. My mental barrier was made of titanium.

Bee came into my room, bringing lunch with her. We sat down, eating roast chicken, salad and local bread. It tasted good. She told me that she was going to take me back to my room, so that I could pick up a few toiletries and clothes. She assured me that Wingnut was no longer there: he was being questioned by Blackwater and the MPs.

After lunch, I cautiously headed back to my trailer with Bee. Spoon was sitting outside his room, along with another member of my Red Zone team. I don't know if they knew what had happened, but they said hello and acted as though they knew nothing. I opened up my door and instantly the smell of alcohol hit me. There was a cup full of booze sitting on my bedside table. I didn't know if it was Wingnut's or mine, but instantly I felt sick and disgusting. I grabbed the cup and poured its contents down the sink.

If only it were that easy to rid myself of the humiliation I was feeling. I quickly grabbed my stuff, and then got out, locking the door behind me. There was no way I'd go back into that room if I could help it. Bee grabbed my computer for me, and we drove back to her compound in silence. She had to go to her office so I made myself comfortable in my temporary accommodation. Slowly and methodically, I began to write my statement, recording what had happened, as best as I could remember.

There were lots of blanks, but I was adamant about certain things. I only poured the first three drinks. After that, Wingnut poured the drinks. I only recall drinking twice more that night, before I was suddenly sick. Wingnut raped me, of that I was certain. I saw his face in the moonlight and I could smell his cigarette stench. He was an ugly troll; there was no way I'd ever encourage his 'attentions'. He was a predator.

*

I stayed with Bee for the next week, but I was eager to return to work and get some normality back into my life. I was sick of sitting around, feeling sorry myself. I didn't want to go home to Australia. I just wanted to immerse myself in my work. Wingnut had closed up and was not saying anything to anyone. He wouldn't confirm or deny what had happened. Blackwater decided to fire him and send him back to the US, pending an investigation into his actions. Until then, he was placed 'under escort' at the team headquarters.

I was finally permitted to return to work. Only a few people, including Jar Jar, knew what had happened. It was kept secret from the rest of the team. Jar Jar gave me a big hug and welcomed me back to the job before I drove him to his first appointment of the day. I was going to get over this ordeal. I just needed to throw myself into my job, and concentrate on what I knew best: client protection.

I was healing. Day by day, I focused on my job, and I delivered results. My clients were pleased with my work, my company promoted me to site leader, taking over from Spoon, and I started inducting new members into team operations in the Green Zone. Professionally, I was getting a lot of satisfaction.

Nobody knew, though, that I couldn't sleep at night without the light on. No one knew I was having nightmares about my teammates coming in and forcing themselves on me. No one knew it was two in the morning before I'd finally fall asleep, exhausted from thinking too much. There was no way I was ever going to admit that I had sleeping problems as a result of my rape. There was no way I was ever going to admit I had any kind of problem as a result of my rape.

Two months into my rotation I hooked up with Josh, the biggest, baddest, fiercest-looking security bloke I could find, and slowly I began to win back control of my body. With Josh in my life, I felt a little safer at night. I was determined not to be afraid of having a relationship with a man again. I didn't want to fear being intimate with someone just because my body had been ravaged. I didn't want to be a victim. It sucked.

Josh used to be a sniper in the Australian Army, but left to take up security work with URG. He was exceptionally buff (from many hours spent in the gym), and his entire body was covered in tattoos. Rather than look 'dirty' and horrid, his tattoos were quite artistic yet menacing. It was not a serious union, and I knew I would never find lasting love with him. We were complete opposites. I was straight as an arrow, and he was, well, bent. But he filled a deep void that was in my soul. He knew of my attack, and often we'd talk about how our relationship was 'therapy'. He helped me to win back confidence in my body and myself, without getting too seriously attached. He provided light-hearted conversation and we'd lie in bed for hours just listening to music. Flings aren't always for the best, but our relationship certainly helped me to heal from within.

By the time our affair ended, I was able to sleep with the light off. My nightmares stopped, and I was filled with a renewed sense of self-worth. Several of my friends, and other people I knew, offered to 'do a job' on Wingnut. The offer was tempting, don't get me wrong, but it wouldn't change what had happened. Retribution would come to him eventually. That's how karma works. When it hit him, I hoped it would hit him hard.

The rest of my time Iraq sailed by. On one of my last nights there, Skippy came over and invited me to a barbecue. I didn't want to go. In fact, I had declined every offer he made after I was raped. I didn't want to socialise or talk to people; I just wanted to be by myself. But he was far too convincing this time. It was my second-last night in Iraq and he told me I was duty-bound to attend. Skippy said they were going to light a small bonfire and just have a few quiet drinks – and that he'd be cooking those fabulous steaks he was renowned for. How could I resist?

I arrived at the barbecue very late. I really wasn't in the mood for it, but it would have been rude of me not to turn up. There were only a couple of people left by the time I arrived. Skippy grabbed me a beer, and I sat down in front of the fire. It was nice. Music played in the background, and Skippy began to tell the first of many jokes.

I noticed a guy walking towards us. I just assumed he was another security guy coming over for a few quiet drinks. He was tall, dark and built like Arnold Schwarzenegger. As he walked over, he clocked me sitting in front of the fire. Instantly, I looked away from him. I didn't want to get drawn into his gaze.

He was just another hot-looking security guy as far as I was concerned. They were a dime a dozen over there. I didn't want to get to know him. I didn't want to get involved. I wasn't looking for a relationship. I'd experienced enough in this past year in Iraq to last me a lifetime. I was going home. I just wanted to see my boy again. If I engaged this handsome stranger in conversation, I'd probably fall for him. I didn't want that to happen. Security guys might be hot, but they're not very good at steady relationships.

I spent the night trying to avoid him. I wasn't going to fall for his chiselled good looks and huge muscles. I wasn't going to lose myself in his deep blue eyes or be caught off guard by his sense of humour. Fate was not going to set me up for failure again. Too often she had wielded her power over me. Tonight I would not let her win.

If I'd listened hard enough, I probably would have heard her laughing at my feeble attempts to avoid Paul. It was his birthday. He had arrived back in the country only to be coerced into attending the barbecue by his mates. He also wasn't keen on attending, as he was feeling the effects of jet lag. But his mates wouldn't let him rest. It was his birthday. He had to celebrate.

So he'd also made his way up to the barbecue area, noting the way I quickly looked away from him as he approached. He could sense that I was reserved, but that only sparked his interest in me. He made small talk with his friends, had a few drinks, then, very casually, sidled up to me and introduced himself.

As the night wore on, I began to fall under his spell. I tried to resist him, God knows I did, but it wasn't to be. Skippy began to get rowdy, and eventually burnt his penis on the fire (don't ask me how it happened; just know it was a typical Skippy escapade). I told the guys I'd walk over to the trailers so that they could check out Skippy to make sure it was okay. Paul said he'd join me. Skippy had consumed quite a few drinks by then, and I doubted he could feel much pain. I suggested Paul's mate, Silver Fox, take a look at his penis to make sure he wasn't badly burnt. I knew what it felt like to burn your private parts; it's not much fun!

As we walked to the trailers, and I was giggling about Skippy's situation, Paul suddenly pulled me in close. He wrapped his arms around me, bent his head down to mine, and planted a sweet, soft kiss on my lips. I felt myself melt into his body. He pulled his lips away, and looked deeply into my eyes. My fate was sealed with that kiss. It was the most tender, loving, sensual kiss I'd ever received in my life. We kissed again, more passionately this time. I wrapped my arms around his neck, and drew him close to me. I was in heaven. This was paradise.

Finally, we parted and returned to the group. Skippy was okay and would live to fight another day. Things began to wind down around midnight. Paul walked me to my trailer, kissed me goodnight, and returned to his room. Okay, maybe a little more kissing and talking and holding and sleeping and whatever happened before he left. But I wouldn't want to kiss and tell!

I met up with Paul the next evening, and we talked for hours. He told me about his life before Iraq, his work and his family life. He was separated from his wife, had two children and came from Perth. As I listened to him talk, I grew fonder and fonder of him. I told him about my life, my son and my dreams. I don't think I'd ever revealed so much about myself to another person, but Paul made me feel completely comfortable.

I was very upfront with him. I told him I did not want to start anything with him, as I was just about to leave the country. I didn't want to use him or be used. I was enjoying his company, but

I still didn't know if I could trust him. He understood my reasons, although I could see he was disappointed. Even though I was a little upset myself, I had to protect my heart and my mind. I had made a secret pact with myself before I'd even met him, that if any guy were truly and honestly interested in me, they would go to the effort of making things work. That was the sort of man I'd want in my life.

On my last day in Iraq, Paul sent me a goodbye text message as I left for the Blackwater house. The team there was going to take me and a few other contractors out to the BIAP to catch our flights home. After receiving orders and packing my equipment onto the truck, I positioned myself inside the commander's armoured vehicle.

The commander's vehicle was situated second in the convoy. We headed out of the Green Zone, 'rolling hard, rolling heavy'. I felt completely safe in the commander's capable hands, but was ready for action nevertheless. We weren't very far along Route Irish when suddenly an explosion erupted next to our vehicle. Everyone braced themselves.

We were coming off an overpass at the time. The first vehicle made it safely off, but the roadside bomb exploded just as we passed by it. The vehicle shook and swerved to the side. I readied myself for the ensuing small-arms fire, but there was none. The rest of the convoy made it safely off the ramp, and we continued along Route Irish.

After arriving at Baghdad airport safely, we had a quick debrief about the attack. Some thought that the explosion was the US military conducting a 'controlled detonation'. They were only doing them at certain times, and this bomb hadn't gone off in that time period. The IED had gone off within 8 metres of our vehicle. The US army certainly wouldn't detonate a bomb within metres of a passing Blackwater team. But insurgents would.

It was later confirmed that insurgents had indeed attempted to blow us up that day. It was believed that the insurgent IED was faulty or not set up correctly, and so the explosion was not lethal enough to inflict damage on us. Perhaps that's why it wasn't followed up with small-arms fire. None of the vehicles was disabled so the enemy would have had to fend off five vehicles with heavy machine-gun fire if they had tried.

Forty-eight hours later, I arrived home to Kane and embraced him in my arms. I felt normal. I felt good. I felt all the ravages of war seeping out of my mind. I was back with my little boy, and I was going to give him a holiday he'd never forget. I was going to give Bruce, Pamela and all their family a holiday they'd never forget. Three weeks later, we all left for the Gold Coast.

In late December, I paid for everyone to fly to the Gold Coast for a theme-park holiday. We swam with the dolphins, went down the waterslides and shopped at all the big centres. We ate at restaurants, went sightseeing and bonded as an 'extended family'. It was a fabulous holiday. It was money well spent. I know Kane and I had a great time, and I'm sure Bruce's family did too.

In return, Bruce invited me to his brother's house, located a few hours from Canberra. We were going to spend the New Year's holiday with them. It was while I was there that I found myself thinking about Paul. I had not sent him many emails, as I'd been busy with my family. The emails I had sent him were light-hearted and impersonal. I woke up on New Year's morning thinking that I would make the first step to see if Paul really wanted to pursue things with me. It had been at least a couple of weeks since we last wrote to each other.

When we returned to Canberra, I logged onto my computer, not really knowing what I would write to Paul. As it turned out, there was an email waiting for me from him. It was as if he had read my thoughts and knew exactly what I wanted from him. I wrote him a long letter back, and, from there, things steadily progressed.

While on holidays, I managed to break my little toe. I broke it right off the bone and was forced to hobble around on crutches for the next couple of weeks. I didn't let it stop me from buying a little townhouse in Canberra, though. I had made enough money to pay a 20 per cent deposit, stamp duty and all the other associated fees for a new house. It was in the same suburb as Bruce's house, and wasn't far from Kane's school. There was some fighting between Bruce and me about where Kane would live. I thought things might degrade between the two of us again. Luckily, we were able to talk through our issues, and finally settle on arrangements for Kane's care.

Kane would live with both of us. He'd spend a week at his dad's, and then a week with me. He would alternate between our two homes. This routine worked well. My relationship with Bruce and Pamela was going on strong, so Kane's welfare was not disrupted. I'd invite Bruce and Pamela over for dinner parties, and I would go over to their house for coffee, a chat, or just to say hello. Things were brilliant between us all.

I told Bruce that I would probably do one more rotation in Iraq, to acquire a good sum to have as savings in the bank, before finally settling down into a normal job. I was keen to meet up with Paul as well. I wanted to see where things were headed with him. I was excited yet nervous about returning. What would this rotation hold for me?

It turned out to be the 'love rotation'. I returned to Iraq's Green Zone. This time I was responsible for looking after two female clients from the former Yugoslavia, and they were great. They always gave me notice if they needed to go somewhere. They often went the gym so I was able to go with them and get regular exercise myself. They hardly ever went out partying, which meant I didn't have to stay up late, waiting to pick them up.

They were courteous and pleasant and loved to chat to me about the 'hot security guys' they were interested in. I couldn't have asked for better clients! My love-life took a radical step. Paul swept me off my feet and they still haven't touched the ground. Every night we'd stay up talking about anything and everything. With no TV or other distractions, the time we spent together was filled with getting to know each other and talking about our dreams for the future.

We spoke about the heartache, the pain and all the crap we'd endured during lives, and we laughed about the funny, happy and joyous moments. I felt like I had met a male version of myself. He understood everything I said, and I understood him too. We were different, yet we were connected. Then one night, Paul told me loved me and said he wanted to spend the rest of his life with me. I was over the moon. I was determined not to say the L-word before he did. I melted as soon as he said it. I knew I was in love with him as well, and, two nights later, I also professed my love to him.

Our first intimate night together felt like heaven. It was how I'd dreamed my wedding night would be. I was shy and nervous, but I was also filled with excitement. When we came together at night, we were like one body fused together. The passion and the love flowed through our veins. We were completely and utterly in love. My life had new meaning because I knew I was going to spend the rest of it with him.

By day, we were high-speed, high-powered security contractors, and by night we were lovers and friends. Even now I smile as I remember the times we furiously threw our webbing, body armour, rifles and pistols into a heap on the floor in a pique of mad passion. It was like a scene out of a movie. We just wanted to be intimate and close with each other. We were crazy for each other, like a couple of lovesick teenagers.

For the first couple of weeks I was back in the country, there was a problem with my ID card. It had expired. Unfortunately, it took time to get a new one issued, and that meant I couldn't do my job or get paid. There I was, technically having a holiday in Iraq. I couldn't eat in any of the food halls or go anywhere in the Green Zone. I was on lockdown. Paul brought me food every day and made sure I had everything I could possibly need.

Was it wise to make plans to spend the rest of my life with Paul while living in the boiling cauldron of war and insurgency? Maybe. Maybe not. But doubt and indecision weren't going to stop me from trying. Paul was from Perth and I was from Canberra. All of Paul's family, friends and his children were in Perth. My family were scattered all around Australia, as were my friends. After I'd thought about it for a long time, it seemed to make more sense for Kane and I to move to Perth than the other way around.

I left Iraq for the final time and tentatively broached the subject with Bruce about moving to Perth. As I expected, Bruce wasn't happy. He didn't want Kane to leave with me. I tried to negotiate every possible option for sharing Kane's care, but Bruce wasn't interested in making any deals. I suggested every option from Kane's spending two years with Bruce and two years with me, to letting Kane decide for himself. It was like talking to a wall: Bruce wasn't interested in talking about it at all.

I guess that is what hurt the most. That we'd worked hard to build up a friendship, and, in the end, it counted for nothing. There was to be no discussion. It was either his way or we'd go to court. Bruce wrote an affidavit against me. Everything I'd ever said and done was turned and used against me. I understood why he was doing it – he didn't want to lose his little boy – but it didn't make the situation any better.

I couldn't bring myself to write an affidavit against him. I had experienced far too much in life to sink to that sort of tit-for-tat level. I couldn't let things continue the way they were, either. With his parents' relationship at a new low point, Kane was beginning to feel the effects. I hated seeing Kane having to deal with an ongoing war between Bruce and me; I knew I had to end his pain. I told Bruce that I would go to Perth, and Kane could stay in Canberra with him. The current family laws would not have allowed me to remove Kane from the state without Bruce's consent. He was never going to give it.

I couldn't stay in Canberra and contribute to Kane's pain. I couldn't let him continue to go through that hell. I loved him too much. It killed me inside, but I had to leave in order for him to heal. If I had stayed, his behaviour probably would have worsened. I felt utterly betrayed by Bruce. First he broke my heart, and then he took my son from me.

To make things worse, I was informed by the US Justice Department that Wingnut was going to get away with his crime. There wasn't enough evidence to convict him, and they had to drop the charges. He alleged that I consented to having sex with him that night. "How could I consent?" I told the solicitor. "I was passed out on my bed. What is consensual about that?" She empathised with me, but as no blood alcohol test was conducted on me, it was hard to prove. I told her I didn't care how much I was grilled on the witness stand, I wanted my day in court. I didn't want him to go free without a fight.

The choice was not mine. The Justice Department gets to decide whether you can take a complaint to court. I was not even given the chance to tell the world what he had done to me. He had done it three times before. Unfortunately, none of the other cases made it to court either. The first woman 'disappeared', the second one dropped the charges, and the third could not get enough evidence against him. The attacks had taken place under similar circumstances. He was an opportunistic, serial rapist and he was getting away with violating women. Who else would he hurt in the years to come?

There was nothing I could do about the situation. While my wounds had healed, nothing could ever wipe away the memory he left with me. God help him if I ever saw his face again. The ugly troll was safe to go back to his wife and four children: none of them the wiser, none of them ever knowing the truth.

Over the next few months, Paul was with me. I spoke to him every night, discussing the good and the bad things going on in our lives. He was still working in Iraq so we communicated via emails and phone calls. He helped me to deal with the pain, and forge a positive future. My experience had taught me that if you were upset or depressed, you had to do whatever it took to get yourself out of that situation. For me, that meant leaving my son with his father. In late January 2007, I organised my move to Perth.

Then, out of the blue, I received an email from Bruce. I read it. Then I re-read it. My head went all dizzy. I couldn't believe what I was reading. To cut a long story short, his marriage was over and he was going to let me take Kane to Perth. I couldn't believe it! He was letting me take Kane. I cried tears of joy.

Oh my God! Bruce was going to let me take Kane. I had endured a druggie boyfriend, and had made it through the most demanding training institution in Australia. I'd had my heart broken, had it cut to pieces and then found strength in a new career. Little did I know that the career would lead to danger and death. My life became tarnished through my association with bad boys and their lust for sex, drugs, alcohol and guns. Then to almost lose my son in a custody battle, it was almost too much to bear.

Now I was going to move to Perth to live with the man of my dreams. My son was going to be right by my side. No more travel. No more guns. No more fighting. I was going to have a quiet life. I was going to live in a suburb surrounded by golf courses and beaches, with normal, beautiful, friendly people. My dreams were finally coming true.

EPILOGUE

I always knew that I would have to hold on and fight for a better future. I knew that I had to hang in there. Bad stuff can't happen forever. Eventually, I was going to have some good luck come my way.

I felt so sorry for Bruce when I heard of his marriage break-up. I offered him my home and my help if he needed it. I took back each and every bad thought I'd had about him, and just felt compassion for what he must have been going through. I knew what that heartache was like. It hurt like hell. We agreed that Kane would stay with him during school holidays, and I promised myself I'd let Kane move back there if he wasn't happy in Perth.

As for me, I am enjoying a happy life. My son has settled into school, and is enjoying his new friends and his new life.

Paul has opened my heart and my mind to all of life's fabulous possibilities. He has made my eyes sparkle again, and has brought me more joy than I ever thought imaginable. While we may have the odd fight, nothing will ever stop me from loving him with all my heart.

Fate has shown me her cruel, heartbreaking, deadly side, but I could not let it destroy me. Life is full of heartbreak. Life is full of challenges and sadness. It is how we deal with what we are handed that makes us who we are. We can either succumb to the pain of it all, or fight for a better future. I chose to fight. The battle was long and filled with hurt, but the prize was well worth the cost.

I now have the best life I could have ever possibly hoped for. I have a home. I have a family. I am married to a man I love and we have three beautiful children between us.

Who knows what the future holds now? With Paul and our children by my side, I know that I can face anything.

ABBREVIATIONS

4 Fd Regt	4 Field Regiment
Acting CM	acting country manager
BIAP	Baghdad International Airport
CPP	close personal protection
CAT	counter assault team
CC	Convention Center
CSH	Combat Support Hospital
EOD	explosive ordnance detection
DOD	US Department of Defense
ID	identification
IED	improvised explosive device
IRI	International Republican Institute
MP	military police
PNG	Papua New Guinea
PT	physical training
PTI	physical training instructor
PSD	private security detail
PX	post exchange
RAAF	Royal Australian Air Force

RAP	Regimental Aid Post
RSO	regional security officer
RPG	rocket-propelled grenade
RMC	Royal Military College
SAT	security advance team
URG	Unity Resources Group

ACKNOWLEDGMENTS

Firstly, I would like to thank my husband, Paul, for all the support and encouragement he has given me over the years. Without his persistence – or obsessive insistence – it might have been another ten years before this book was published.

I would also like to thank the Silver Fox for messing around with destiny and setting Paul and me up to fall in love on that fateful night in Baghdad. And Skippy, thank you for burning your penis and providing us with the opportunity to be alone. (I do hope everything is okay down there now.)

Thanks to my friends from Team Apollo, in particular Outpatient, Wolf, Cobra, Horse, Dr Evil, Ali, Buster and Bee. Your ongoing friendship has meant the world to me. Outpatient, you're a legend. Wolf, I hope this book helps dispel the myths that the haters have believed for so long.

To my Blackwater crew – Diablo, Church, Scooter, Butters, Cowboy, T Boy, Spoon, 86, Bram and Yogi: thanks for the memories, and for your professionalism when on missions.

Thanks to the Blackwater Mamba team – roll hard, roll heavy!

To the 'black ops' team: no ice-cream has ever come close to tasting as good as what we had that night.

Teamwork and leadership have played a major role in my story. As corny as it might sound, thanks to the Australian Army for its quality training, strong ethics and exceptional defence personnel. I was proud to serve my country. Thank you, Major Murray Heron and Leo Legend, for believing in me and inspiring me to be the best that I can be.

I want to thank my mum and dad for all the experiences I was provided with throughout my childhood (except for the ones where I got in trouble).

Dad, thanks for brainwashing me with your 'straight as an arrow' values system and your incredible work ethic. I am truly grateful that you taught me the importance of being honest and doing a job properly.

Mum, thanks for giving me the freedom to explore and participate in 'male' sports and activities. Thanks for teaching me how to be a mum, and for helping me in the times when I was alone and struggling with Kane.

Kane, thanks for being the best little kid a mum could want (note 'little' kid – this teenage thing is not so fun). I hope you grow up never wanting to work in the private security industry, and instead go on to have a stellar career in the NRL.

I'd like to thank my siblings, Ced, Lil, Shannon and Naomi. Our relationship has shaped me and influenced my decisions in life, and for that I am indebted to you.

Thank you to my dear friend Pauline Sanders. Your friendship, support, enthusiasm and zest have been critical to my success. Reaching for the stars is far easier when you have a friend holding you up to the sky.

I would like to thank authors Robert Schofield and Michael John Barnes for feeding my caffeine addiction at coffee shops and for all the advice they gave about getting my book published. And thank you so much for introducing me to my agent, George Karlov.

To George: thank you for believing in my story and for fighting tooth and nail to get it published. After eight years of feeling rejected, you brought my story back to life and made my dream a reality. Your professionalism, determination and enthusiasm have been a godsend, and your sharp humour has made the journey enjoyable. You are the best!

To my publishers at Black Inc. and Nero Books: thanks for publishing a book about an unknown chick doing an unknown job in a world that most people didn't know existed. It has been a pleasure working with the team, in particular Bridget Maidment, who did an outstanding job editing my work.

Thanks to the creative team who designed the book cover: photographer Francis Andrijich, make-up artist Gail Wilton, and Black Inc.'s Peter Long. You turned this old soldier into a Battle Barbie – and that's no easy feat!

Finally, I want to acknowledge all the private security contractors who are still working in the industry. You will never be thanked, you will never be honoured, you will never be remembered for your achievements. Your military service will be forgotten, you'll be labelled mercenaries, and your heroism on the battlefield will never be known. But you do an important job bringing stability to war-torn countries.

Industry regulation and legislation is the only way forward. It will provide protection for your professional reputation, it will act as a guideline for security operations overseas, and it will ratify the important work that private military companies do for legitimate governments.